Who Dies Fighting

Angus Rose

Who Dies Fighting

A Personal Account of the War in Malaya & the Fall
of Singapore, 1942, During the Second World War

Angus Rose

LEONAUR

Who Dies Fighting
A Personal Account of the War in Malaya & the Fall of Singapore, 1942,
During the Second World War
by Angus Rose

First published under the title
Who Dies Fighting

Leonaur is an imprint of Oakpast Ltd

ISBN: 978-1-78282-642-2 (hardcover)
ISBN: 978-1-78282-643-9 (softcover)

http://www.leonaur.com

Publisher's Notes

Contents

Angus Rose

An Introduction by the Leonaur Editors

Our perception of the past is similar to visual perspective. Events, irrespective of their original magnitude, simplify as they drift away on an ever condensing timeline. The most significant historical events become either broadly famous or notorious as their details coalesce (rarely accurately) until a synopsis of them can be written in a few lines. For many living today the Second World War, concluded less than eighty years ago, has not only been consigned to history books, but has always resided there. For younger generations, this monumental conflict has little bearing on the modern world as they know it. Now that those who fought in it are fading away this has become an inevitability. In fact, far more recent conflicts have already begun to be vague, misunderstood or forgotten.

The most noteworthy events of conflicts are no more immune from the distortions of time. The collective memory responds better, of course, to a resounding victory. So 'The Battle of Britain', 'The D-Day Invasion of Normandy' and some others are held longer and with greater affection in popular recollection than a tenacious defence such as 'The Battle of Kohima'. 'The Evacuation from Dunkirk' is redeemed nostalgically as a magnificent achievement snatched from the jaws of defeat. Defeats themselves, unless one of the protagonists is heroically annihilated like the Spartans at Thermopylae, perhaps unsurprisingly fare the least well in history or in popular memory.

Military defeats assume by degrees, irrespective of their details, a collective responsibility on the part of everyone involved in them and are rarely commemorated. Their causes should ideally be straightforward and the result of criminal negligence or arrant stupidity on the part of the defeated commander rather than upon any military genius or prowess on the part of his victorious counterpart and the forces under his command. Thus, verdicts upon them may be made quickly, dismissively and their memories smartly swept under the carpet of history. That which might be considered 'fair' has very little bearing on the matter.

This book concerns (as its much broader canvas) a defeat on a grand scale that was the conquest of Malaya and ultimately the capture of the island of Singapore in 1941–42 by Japanese forces as they swept westwards to overwhelm the outposts of the British Empire in the Far East.

Coincidentally, this writer belongs to one of the first British post-war generations and his father served with the Royal Air Force in the Far East during the Second World War so lived through the days of the events described in these pages. His father's verdict on the cause of the fall of Singapore was, 'Singapore fell because the guns to defend it were mounted pointing in the 'wrong' direction, facing out to sea, could not be moved and that was not the direction from which the Japanese attacked'. One assumed that the Japanese selected this tactic precisely because the guns were foolishly 'facing the wrong direction'. This was not an original or uncommon perspective of the fall of one of the empire's most formidable bastions. Indeed, it is an abiding popular view no doubt originating long before this writer heard it as a boy a little more than a decade after VJ Day. However, this serves to underline how quickly a single dimensional view of a defeat is broadcast and so can gain provenance. Since the fall of Malaya was an unquestionable disaster for the British it is reasonable to speculate that there has been only moderate interest in its study. Winston Churchill said, 'A defeat is one thing, but a disgrace is another'. It should be recognised, however, that it is tempting to relegate a defeat to a humiliation whether the facts warrant such a verdict or not.

This book is not a history of the Malayan Campaign and does not purport to be one. It is a personal account, written during wartime by a remarkable British officer imbued with the kind of warrior spirit that motivated (in an unconnected way) David Stirling, during much the same period as the events described in these pages, to create the SAS in the Western Desert. Its singularity lies in the fact that very few people are aware that these kinds of military operations were being planned and undertaken by British forces at this stage of the war in Malaya against the Japanese. Nevertheless, the campaign in Malaya is the canvas upon which Angus Rose's story is painted and the benefit of time and hindsight enables us to examine the events which give the intimate narrative of this book context.

The two principal aggressors of the Second World War had more in common than might be readily imagined. Both Germany and Japan were newcomers to modern nationhood. The strongest German state, Prussia had for ages struggled against the dominance of its neighbours, France and Russia. Through the small European wars of the later 19th century it gathered power, influence and ultimately hegemony over its smaller brethren states until it became the foundation stone of a modern German nation.

In the same period Japan wrenched itself against violent internal opposition from virtual medieval isolationism into the modern world. By the turn of the 20th century it was in conflict with Russia. The naval battles of the Russo-Japanese War were the first great sea battles of the age of the modern battleships and many contemporary commentators believed the Russians would deliver a harsh lesson to an upstart nation that had never been, despite its island homelands, a sea-going power. Exactly the opposite proved to be the case. These naval victories, particularly 'The Battle of Tsushima' inspired in the Japanese a conviction that, despite its infancy as a modern nation, the potentials for imperial power which would dominate the South-East Asian region were at hand.

The First World War 1914-18, came about inexorably and inevitably. The Kaiser's ironic question, 'When shall we have our place in the sun?' revealed that Germany knew the business of global empire building had placed practically all of its rewards in the hands of the world's long-established powers. The time was past when new advantages could be forged from unexploited potentials and henceforth the benefits of imperialism would need to be wrested from the grasp of others by force of arms.

In the East the Japanese, in a similar position, turned their attention towards China. During the First World War, Japanese troops and naval warships within an Anglo-Japanese task force took a significant role in the fall of the German held port of Tsingtao in 1914. An American observer declared that the action was clearly a constituent part of Japan's own interventionist designs in China. Japan had gone to war with China over Korea at the turn of the century and by 1937 Japanese forces were once again engaged in China in a conflict that would only come to an end with the conclusion of the Second World War.

In 1941 the British Empire and its Commonwealth were once again desperately engaged in total war with an unfulfilled Germany and had become familiar with Japan's ongoing but remote operations against the Chinese which were in their fourth year. Only the farthest eastern outposts of European colonisation bordered Japan's influence. British military intelligence in the region was not so remiss that it was unaware of the potential dangers posed by the Japanese, the attractions of natural resources in the region in the hands of western powers or that the Japanese were mustering a massive military force destined to be deployed in a significant campaign somewhere by November 1941. Concerns provoked demands that Japan clarify its intentions. The Japanese, not entirely implausibly, replied that these activities were contiguous to their established campaign in China.

Within weeks, on the 8th of December, 1941, having occupied Indo-China the Japanese invasion of the Malayan peninsula began through Thailand. Notably this happened less than 24 hours after an arguably more renowned 'day of infamy', December 7th, 1941 when the Japanese launched a surprise air attack from a carrier fleet upon the United States of America's Pacific Fleet anchored at peace in Pearl Harbor.

Clearly the Japanese had long planned these operations, which were obviously only the first moves in a more expansive strategy, and so had substantially resourced them for combat on land, sea and in the air to overwhelm any military opposition which would be on a peace time standing. These attacks were launched with no diplomatic preamble which might alert an enemy as to their true intentions. Even the harshest critic would acknowledge that such an invasion would place its recipient at a severe disadvantage and compel it in the first instance to act defensively. For the British the fact that they were also engaged in a war elsewhere they were not winning and which required the majority of the nation's military resources was a paramount consideration. Malaya Command was under resourced in every way (except in quantities of men) and had no expectation that its situation would be remedied.

Soldiers are fated to be those who actually lose battles and that makes them ideal candidates for being held responsible for defeats. Major-General William Dobbie, General Officer Commanding in Malaya from 1937-39 accurately predicted how the Malayan penin-

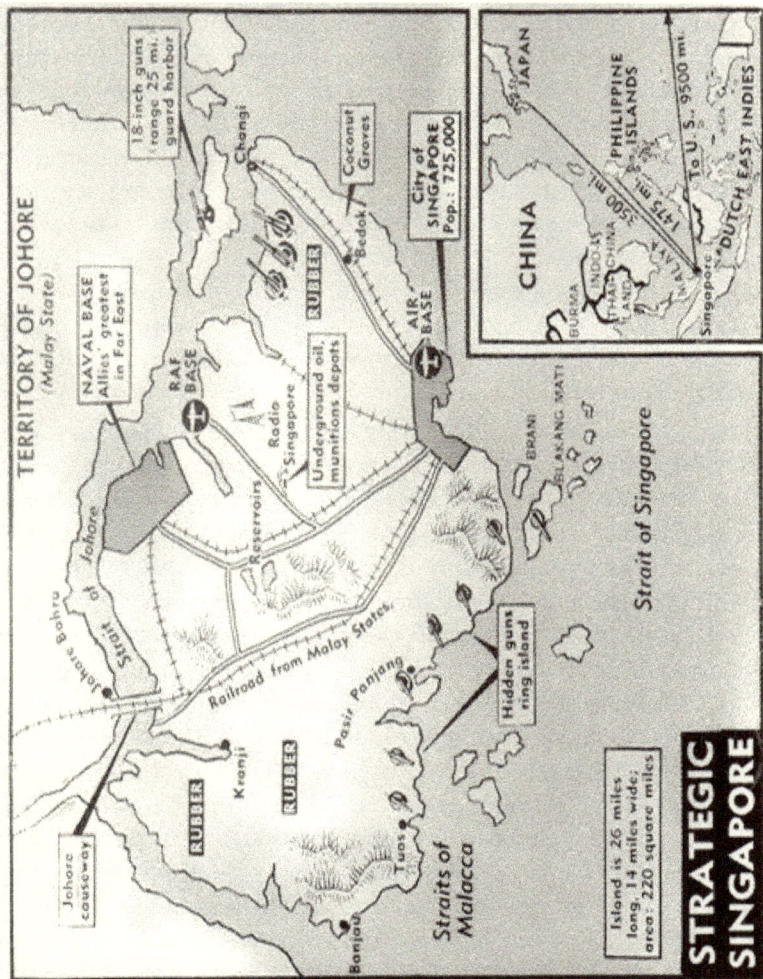

STRATEGIC SINGAPORE

TERRITORY OF JOHORE
(Malay State)

18-inch guns
range 25 mi.
guard harbor

Coconut Groves

City of
SINGAPORE
Pop.: 725,000

NAVAL BASE
Allies' greatest
in Far East

RAF
BASE

AIR
BASE

Radio
Singapore

Underground oil,
munitions depots

Reservoirs

Railroad from Malay States.

RUBBER

Changi

Bedok

RUBBER

Johore Bahru

Strait of Johore

Johore
causeway

Kranji

RUBBER

RUBBER

Tuas

Banjou

Pasir Panjang

Straits of
Malacca

Hidden guns
ring island

BRANI

BLAKANG MATI

Strait of Singapore

Island is 26 miles
long, 14 miles wide;
area: 220 square miles

CHINA

JAPAN

BURMA

INDO-CHINA

THAILAND

PHILIPPINE
ISLANDS

MALAYA

DUTCH EAST INDIES

Singapore

1500 mi.

1475 mi.

To U.S. 9500 mi.

sula would be invaded by Japan should that eventuality ever actually occur. So, when the attack finally came its form came as no surprise to anyone who had read the documents on the matter. The person tasked by Dobbie to prepare this tactical risk assessment was his Chief Staff Officer, a certain Arthur Ernest Percival who would in due course reappear in the story of the Malayan Campaign.

It was hardly unprecedented that the British Government ignored the military conclusions of its leading military men. The issue was one of perspective. Dobbie rightly viewed the territory for which he was responsible as a prospective battleground. The British Government, responsible for administering an empire, viewed the situation globally. Malaya was an imperial holding protected by a strong naval base at Singapore servicing a Royal Navy fleet with responsibilities which included the security of the seaways to Australasia. However, by 1940 Lieutenant-General Lionel Bond commanding the British Army in Malaya at the time knew that the island of Singapore itself would never be seen as a deterrent which would prevent the entire Malayan peninsula from invasion.

The guns of fortress Singapore which became emblematic of the entire defeat were indeed mostly sited on the seaward sides of the island. Only the most hopeful strategist might expect that an amphibious assault would be obligingly launched from the sea given the existence of any number of better offensive options. In any event amphibious assaults were not commonplace at this stage in the war. There had been one small scale landing by British commandos on a Mediterranean island earlier in 1941: a fact, as will be discovered, which coincidentally bears on Angus Rose's story. For the most recent experience, of the large scale amphibious assaults against determined opposition, planners would need to look to the First World War. The landings at Gallipoli and Tanga did not deliver outcomes which would have encouraged an enemy to attempt such an assault directly upon Singapore. In the final analysis one may only question whether the influence of the Singapore fortress guns, which could be turned to fire landward but were supplied from an arsenal of armour piercing shells intended for naval targets, would have ultimately saved the island given that the Japanese had massive air superiority and that Malaya itself had already fallen.

The story of the fall of Malaya and Singapore cannot be told without the re-introduction of Lieutenant-General Arthur Percival who

Lieutenant-General Arthur Percival

arrived in Singapore in April 1941 and was unfortunate to be appointed General Officer Commanding, Malaya Command. It is assessed that Percival presided over the largest capitulation in British military history with in excess of 138,000 British and Commonwealth troops killed, wounded or captured. It is nonsensical to place the entire responsibility for the Malayan disaster upon Percival's shoulders in his eight-month tenure as GOC, Malaya Command especially since he was experiencing the realities of his own predictions made four or five years previously. He knew it was a matter of established government policy, with which he concurred, that interests in the Far East would be subordinated to those in the main theatre of operations and that the majority of resources which would be despatched anywhere would be to Russia and the Middle East.

Whilst Percival had twice the number of troops as the enemy many among them were of poor quality, often untrained and largely inexperienced in battle or indeed not fighting soldiers at all. Significantly, from the perspective of the infantry, the Japanese troops who were experienced and battle hardened had over 250 tanks at their disposal whilst the British and Commonwealth troops had virtually none. The Japanese not only had more than twice the number of aircraft but they were also piloted by trained and battle experienced airmen. British aircraft were not only of poorer quality, but many were quickly destroyed early in the conflict often on the ground. The Japanese also had command of the sea and two capital ships, the Royal Navy's battleship 'HMS Prince of Wales' and the battlecruiser 'HMS Repulse' were quickly sunk in the South China Sea off Kuantan. The effect these considerations had upon the morale of both combatants needs no elaboration. In modern warfare significant superiority in armour, aircraft and sea power will usually doom an enemy especially one lacking effective resupply.

The Japanese plan of attack was nevertheless daring and well executed and the British response to it, simply put, was a series of defensive actions and retreats down the peninsula to Singapore until their backs were quite literally finally against the sea with nowhere to go. Winston Churchill instructed that the defence of the island be protracted but Percival, aware at that point that half of the island was occupied by the Japanese and that the supply of water and ammunition was all but expended, surrendered on February 15th, 1942. The battle for Malaya had lasted a little over two months. Percival was compelled to march in company with an oversized white flag for the benefit of Japanese newsreel cameramen and the image was indelibly recorded for posterity.

From that moment Arthur Percival was also fated to become as emblematic of the British defeat in Malaya as were the redundant Singapore fortress guns. Though we are perpetually encouraged never to judge a book by its cover this is advice universally ignored by practically everyone. Whilst Percival's integrity and personal courage were an established fact (having served through the Great War and been awarded an MC, *Croix de Guerre* and two DSOs) the tall, spare framed, unassuming Percival did not portray the archetypal warrior, but rather the opposite. It is a fact that he had never before commanded an army corps, probable that he was more of a staff officer than a fighting general and would, barring a miracle, certainly have lost Malaya had he been a Wellington.

Fate has placed him in the same theatre of the war as the bulldog-jawed General Bill Slim who appeared to exemplify a military dynamism which promised and delivered victories. Furthermore, the war in the Pacific and in Burma later demonstrated that not only would there never have been an embattled Japanese officer who would have surrendered 130,000 troops under his command to 30,000 enemy troops, there would also never have been a Japanese officer who would have surrendered had the numerical imbalance been reversed. Unimagined at the moment of the surrender, since German POW's had been treated well by the Japanese after Tsingtao in 1914, the subsequent barbaric treatment of British and Commonwealth prisoners of war by the Japanese became a well-documented war crime. The finer points of history may be debated, but whether they are entirely fair or not, these are the burdens Percival's memory has indisputably come to bear.

The Japanese attitude to military service and personal sacrifice for nation and emperor was incomprehensible to the soldiers who fought them, but that it gave the Japanese a decisive advantage in the attack on Malaya against an enemy that had never before experienced it is beyond dispute. The conviction that the Japanese soldier possessed a super human ability as a jungle fighter impossible for western troops to emulate or counter had its foundations in the Malayan Campaign and took some time and much effort to eradicate among citizen soldiers whose idea was to 'do their bit' and go home. Once hard experi-

THE SURRENDER AT SINGAPORE

ence had educated all allied forces as to what they could expect from the Japanese upon the battlefield, or in captivity, attitudes and action on the subject of surrender as that applied to themselves, or the enemy, changed irrevocably. As one of Wingate's Chindits put it after the war, 'They didn't give us a chance and we didn't give them a chance'.

Percival was taken into captivity as a POW, but was rescued from Manchuria by an OSS team in company with the American, General Jonathan Wainwright who was the officer responsible for the surrender of the Philippines to the Japanese. These two officers symbolically stood behind General Douglas MacArthur at the signing of the Japanese surrender aboard the 'USS Missouri' anchored in Tokyo Bay on September 2nd, 1945. Arthur Percival retired from the British Army with his rank of Lieutenant-General. His pension was that of his lower substantive rank of Major-General. He was not, very unusually for an officer of his rank, awarded a knighthood. Jonathan Wainwright was awarded the Medal of Honor, the highest award his nation could bestow upon him.

Readers will appreciate, given the above, how incredible Angus Rose's story is because during a campaign of retreats in which everyone associated with the British command knew the certain outcome would be defeat this officer thought only of taking the fight to the Japanese enemy. Without doubt Angus Rose was the consummate professional soldier. He believed that it was his purpose to literally fight the enemy and he was determined to do it with a simple conviction that did not falter at the most probable consequence given the prevailing circumstances which was that he would be killed in action.

Irrespective of the stifling position he held on Percival's staff, Major Angus Rose of the Argyll and Sutherland Highlanders was to his core an infantry officer and submission to inactivity whilst awaiting the inevitable was an affront to every fibre of his being. Rose began, therefore, to think 'outside the box' of conventional tactics. His original idea to insert a battalion behind the Japanese to disrupt supply lines, relieve pressure on the front and hold his position until relieved by a counter-attack was rejected since no battalions could be spared. The concept bore similarities with Wingate's later Chindit operations in theory though, as it transpired, there would be no counter-attack and on the Malayan peninsular no possible escape route for such a unit making its annihilation certain.

Eventually Rose was given permission to create a raiding unit of mainly Australian volunteer troops which would be transported behind enemy lines by boat and there create as much chaos as possible. This was a high risk gambit which would never influence on the course of the short lived Malayan campaign. The comparative ease by which these troops could be landed on Malaya's long coastline underlines the futility of creating a series of defensive lines down the peninsula which had been suggested and rejected in the past. This strategy may well have been the best worst option, but during the subsequent Italian Campaign the line hopping Anzio and Salerno landings would reveal that ultimately this would not stop a determined and well resourced advance along a peninsula. The subsequent campaign fought and won in the Far East would demonstrate that the only way to secure Malaya was to dominate the entire region which in 1941 was not a remote possibility.

Angus Rose's book is well titled according to his principles which were simply that a fighting man to be true to himself must fight regardless of any other consideration. There is little doubt he was a dangerous man in the style of Michael Calvert of the Chindits and his book contains its share of action and excitement. Some critics may justifiably label Angus Rose as a romantic. Others may view him as admirably brave whilst still others may consider him foolhardy. Certainly, there have been other soldiers who acted according to Angus Rose's idea of soldiering who, dependent on the success or failure of their efforts, have shared these accolades or suffered these censures.

Angus Rose will be a new name to most of the readers of his book. In a campaign where few reputations were enhanced there is little doubt that Rose can hold up his head for he bore himself with integrity according to his own creed. Irrespective of any other verdict on how he chose to fight his war, having turned the final page of 'Who Dies Fighting', Angus Rose will certainly have earned his reader's respect.

Angus Rose survived the war and this new Leonaur edition of his book has been made possible by the support and approval of his family.

The Leonaur Editors, 2017

8 PL A COY 2 A&SH, SINGAPORE 1941 STANDING (LEFT TO RIGHT) : 2ND LT DEREK MONTGOMERY-CAMPBELL, CPL TONY HODGSON, PTE BILL ELLIOTT, PTE ANDY FERGUS, PTE KEN GEE, PTE RICHARD CLARK, PTE JIM MASTERTON, PTE BILL BATEY, PTE ROCKY WANLESS, PTE BILL GRAINGER, PTE GERRY DAVIDSON, 2ND LT GORDON SCHIACH FRONT ROW (LEFT TO RIGHT) : PTE TOMMY FORBES, PTE JACK VENNER, PTE STAN HARRIS, PTE TOMMY HUNTER, L CPL BUD FISHER, PTE BERT BUCKINSON

Still, when a chief dies bravely,
We bind with green one wrist—
Green for the brave, for heroes
One crimson thread we twist.
Say ye, oh gallant Hillmen,
For these, whose life has fled,
Which is the fitting colour,
The green one or the red?
—Sir Francis Hastings Doyle

INTO BATTLE

The naked earth is warm with spring,
And with green grass and bursting trees
Leans to the sun's gaze glorying,
And. quivers in the sunny breeze;
And life is colour and warmth and light,
And a striving evermore for these;
And he is dead who will not fight;
And who dies fighting has increase.

The fighting man shall from the sun.
Take warmth, and life from the glowing earth;
Speed with the light-foot winds to run,
And with the trees to newer birth;
And find, when fighting shall be done,
Great rest, and fullness after dearth.

All the bright company of Heaven
Hold him in their high comradeship,
The Dog-Star, and the Sisters Seven,
Orion's Belt and sworded hip.

The woodland trees that stand together,
They stand to him each one a friend;
They gently speak in the windy weather;
They guide to valley and ridge's end.

The kestrel hovering by day,
And the little owls that call by night,
Bid him be swift and keen as they,
As keen of ear, as swift of sight.

The blackbird, sings to him, 'Brother, brother,
If this be the last song you shall sing,
Sing well, for you may not sing another;
Brother, sing.'

In dreary, doubtful, waiting hours,

Before the brazen frenzy starts,
The horses show him nobler powers;
O patient eyes, courageous hearts!

And when the burning moment breaks,
And all things else are out of mind,
And only joy of battle takes
Him by the throat, and makes him blind;

Through joy and blindness he shall know,
Not caring much to know, that still
Nor lead nor steel shall reach him, so
That it be not the Destined Will.

The thundering line of battle stands,
And in the air death moans and sings;
But Day shall clasp him with strong hands,
And Night shall fold him in soft wings.

—Julian Grenfell

UPPER MALAYA

MAIN ROADS
SECONDARY ROADS
RAILWAYS
JAPANESE ATTACKS
AERODROMES

SIAM

KEDAH

PERLIS
KANGAR
ALOR STAR
GURUN
KOTA BHARU
KUALA TRENGGANU
KUALA KRAI

UNSELECTED INFILTRATION DURING
2ⁿᵈ AND 3ʳᵈ WEEKS OF DEC.

SOUTHERN MALAYA

SINGAPORE AND JOHORE HARBOUR

Angus Rose

Foreword

By Major General David Thomson CB CBE MC
Colonel. The Argyll and Sutherland Highlanders
1992-2000

'Who Dies Fighting' is the story of a man who in late 1941 sought permission from Headquarters Malaya Command to take the fight to the enemy. He then collected men from a variety of units and set out to raid the Japanese lines-of-communication in Malaya. It was a period when Britain could well have been described as losing the war; the Japanese were rampant in the Far East, the United States had been grievously wounded by the attack on Pearl Harbour and had yet to really enter the war, and Britain's problems closer to home made ultimate victory seem unlikely, except possibly in the mind of Winston Churchill.

Angus Rose, an officer of the 93rd Highlanders (The 2nd Battalion The Argyll and Sutherland Highlanders), was detached from his battalion at the time of the majority of his account. He writes with commendable fluency and somehow managed to get permission to publish his book in 1944, whilst the war in the Far East was still raging. Emotions were still running high at this time, not least because many Argylls were still prisoners of the Japanese. Even his outstanding former Commanding Officer and friend, Brigadier Ian Stewart, was not pleased both at some of Angus Rose's criticisms of individuals and his remarks about decisions made under the strain of war.

As the years passed and the prisoners came home, a somewhat different view on 'Who Dies Fighting' emerged. Rose's comments were generally accepted and found to be as accurate as a book written about a retreat could ever be. As far as I know, few other Argylls felt as strongly as Stewart had done and it was in fact another well-known Argyll personality, who had escaped with Rose, Captain David

Wilson, later brigadier, who personally typed out the first draft of this story on the boat during their voyage from Batavia to Ceylon.

In short, few in today's society have had access to the original book and I commend its republication to a new audience who I hope will appreciate just some of the pressures and dramas that Angus Rose records so eloquently.

CHAPTER 1

The Phoney War

In anticipation of a European War, I was enjoying long leave at home during the summer of 1939. Glorious days spent on English cricket fields and paddocks were freely mixed with the glittering nights of the last pre-war London season. Towards the end of July I heard that my regiment, the 2nd Argyll and Sutherland Highlanders, had been dispatched, together with the rest of the 12th Indian Infantry Brigade, from Secunderabad to reinforce the garrison of Singapore. The previous Autumn this same brigade had got to the stage of entraining for Madras when the orders were cancelled on account of the Munich agreement. This time, though, they were to go right through.

I concluded my leave to the accompaniment of the Russo-German Pact, the embodiment of the Territorial Army, the invasion of Poland and the uncorking of all the *Krug* '28 that I could lay my hands on. On September 2nd, I reported for duty at Edinburgh and sailed a few days later from Clydeside, on board the *Duchess of Bedford*. We were in convoy with some eight or nine other ships and, after a month of not uneventful travel, we reached Bombay. As an anti-climax to our voyage, the gangway was initially secured by means of an umbrella handle, deftly manipulated by a Sikh.

Hector Greenfield, my commanding officer, and I were destined for Malaya and, after a week in Bombay, we crossed over to Calcutta and took ship to Singapore where we eventually arrived on October 18th. We found the battalion doubled up with the Loyal Regiment in some palatial barracks in a suburb of the town at Alexandria.

Ian Stewart, our second-in-command, was hotting up the tempo of our training and had made all arrangements for taking the battalion into camp, up country, for jungle warfare exercises. In this respect, we

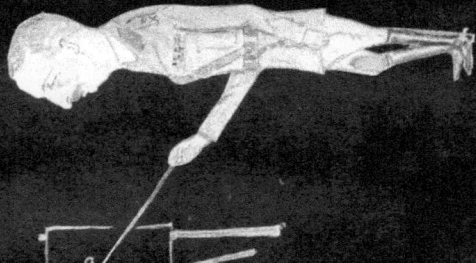

"A FEW WORDS"

received very little encouragement from Malaya Command and they assured us that if we were not drowned in the seasonal rains we would be decimated by malaria. However, as far as Ian was concerned, difficulties of this nature were merely there to be overcome.

At that time the garrison of Malaya Command consisted of the Gordons, the Loyals, the Manchesters and the Malay Regiment. Apart from these infantry units there was the Fixed Defence Artillery, consisting of 15-inch and 9.2-inch guns, a certain amount of heavy ack-ack and the usual complement of fortress troops. In addition to these regular forces there were three battalions of Straits Settlement Volunteers and about five battalions of Federated Malay States Volunteers, but these forces were dispersed all over the countryside and not normally embodied.

Apart from the army, there was an R.A.F. Command consisting of two flying boat squadrons, two torpedo bomber squadrons and two Blenheim bomber squadrons. The navy was represented by various units, including a flotilla of submarines.

The broad outline of the defence scheme was that the R.A.F. and Fixed Defences would sink the Jap transports far out to sea, if the Navy had not already done so, and the infantry would man the open beaches and plug into any Nips that had escaped death in the ocean. Those parts of the island where the shore consisted of mangrove swamps were held to be impassable to infantry and were ruled out of court as possible landing places. This tradition of certain country being 'impassable to infantry' died very hard, although my own battalion gave a practical demonstration, in a fortress exercise, that there was no ground on the island that presented an insurmountable obstacle to determined and well-trained infantry. The Japs gave some similar demonstrations later on.

Generally speaking, the defence of Singapore can best be described as static. Switch lines did exist but, here again, the flanks were secured by purely imaginary obstacles. We made up for our deficiency in troops by substituting a lot of wishful thinking. It had been appreciated, however, that the Japs might land on the beaches at Mersing, which was some hundred miles up country on the east coast, as an alternative to making a direct attack on Singapore itself. At Mersing the beaches gave direct access to the inland communications and, if the Jap succeeded in landing here, he would be able to advance down to the Straits of Johore and attack Singapore from landward.

The task of 12th Indian Infantry Brigade was to oppose any such

IAN STEWART AND ANGUS ROSE

Jap landing at Mersing and, subsequently, to fight a delaying action back along the Mersing-Johore Bahru Road. How the Jap was, eventually, to be driven back into the sea was never quite clear.

In this role, we had a so-called 'last ditch' position at a place called Kota Tinggi and here we constructed a kind of miniature 'Maginot Line'. Laying out the Kota Tinggi line was always an entertaining pastime, as it was invariably done to the accompaniment of Japanese agents. These Nips would follow along behind us taking all the measurements and carefully writing them down in their note-books; so, in order to give the little men more homework, we used to stick in extra pegs. So much for British anti-espionage, although there are a lot more stories that could be told.

Ian had arranged that we should go to Mersing for our training so that we should learn the topography of our battle area and, at the same time, familiarise ourselves with jungle conditions. We did a tactical move to Mersing in motor transport and it was interesting driving through this type of country which was new to all of us. The road went alternatively through symmetrically planted rubber, where visibility would be about the same as in an English orchard, or else through primitive jungle where the forest came right up to the road in one solid block of vegetation. The casual observer got the impression that the whole jungle was one dense mass of impenetrable foliage, but this was not the case.

Along the borders of roads, where the trees had been cut down and light had come in, the jungle grew up again in great density. This was known as secondary jungle. Once inside this narrow belt, which only went to a depth of a score of yards, there was the real, or primary, jungle. It was not normally necessary to cut through primary jungle, except in river courses or over water-logged ground. Primary jungle varied but on an average, I would say visibility would be thirty or forty yards. We would refer to jungle as 'average', 'close' or 'open'. Tourists and office-bound staff officers, who never had time to leave the road, got a completely wrong impression of what jungle really was and 'impenetrable jungle' was, of course, a complete myth.

Apart from the rubber plantations and the primitive jungle, with its numerous sluggish streams, there were a few pineapple estates where visibility was unrestricted.

During this drive, I ruminated as to the type of tactics that one could possibly employ and, at the end of the journey, I was in complete despair. What made it worse was that no one else was any the

TRAINING IN MALAYA

TRAINING IN MALAYA

wiser, although Ian had some enthusiastic ideas. In Singapore jungle warfare, had scarcely been thought of, as the troops on the island fought in beach defences. There was no common tactical doctrine and no one to give us any guidance.

This omission was, however, not peculiar to Malaya Command. In pre-war days, we made no attempt to standardise tactics or to differentiate between the tactics required for specific types of warfare. There was an exception to this rule which concerned mountain warfare against tribesmen, and, in this connection, we had a specialised form of tactics which was studied, taught and practically tested. For the actual task in hand it produced excellent results but, as peace-time tribal scrapping bears no relationship whatsoever to modern European warfare, there were obvious limitations. We also specialised in training for 'Duties in aid of the Civil Power'—a form of operations in which the British soldier was, without exaggeration, second to none.

But from these narrow channels our tactical doctrines flowed into a broad expanse of uncharted ocean. The manuals were pompous, heavy, often platitudinous and otherwise equivocal. The result was that, if anybody had the perseverance and determination to read them (which was no mean feat), they could interpret them in any way they liked. Accordingly, everyone had completely different tactical conceptions, or else none at all. Consequently, officers, particularly in the subordinate ranks, were continually required to modify their tactical creeds to the whims of their immediate superiors (or else to take the consequences), so it was small wonder that we made such modest progress.

Tactics is the technique of closing with and destroying your enemy, and that technique is going to be completely different according to the type of country over which you are going to fight. Broadly speaking there are to my mind six different types: Desert warfare, Mountain warfare, Field and Wood warfare, Jungle warfare, Snow and Ice warfare and Amphibious warfare or Landing operations. To be worth your weight as a soldier you need to be conversant with the technique of all these types. Before the war I knew the technique of Field and Wood warfare, within the bounds of the strictly limited armoury that the British Exchequer had put at my disposal, and I also knew how to conduct my soldiery in the presence of hostile tribesmen discharging musket balls, as I had received practical experience in this particular technique. On the other hand I knew nothing, or next to nothing, about any of the other forms of warfare, simply because I had not been taught. Modern war is a frighteningly complex subject because, apart from the diversity of weapons and technical devices, there is also the diversity of techniques. The whole problem is analogous to ball games. There are lots of them and we may be called upon to represent the country in any given one.

After this digression, it will appear obvious why we should find ourselves in this state of unpreparedness to defend the Malayan jungle; but Ian Stewart wasted no time in rectifying our deficiencies. We started off with a number of dispiriting exercises in which the battalion seemed to disintegrate as soon as it took to the jungle, but, by the end of our six weeks, we had made a certain amount of progress, even if we had only learnt what not to do.

About December the Jap war scare died down, and we returned to Singapore where a newly-constructed hutted camp had been prepared for us opposite the Botanical Gardens, in the suburb of Tanglin. The amenities of Tyersall Park Camp, which was to be our home for the next two years, were pretty crude, but we made it as comfortable as circumstances permitted and, before long, it became impregnated with a regimental atmosphere. The more I see of the world the more convinced I am that it doesn't matter where you are, but what does matter is whom you are with. In this respect, we couldn't have been better off.

A good deal of ragging used to go on in the Mess and, on one particularly good evening, it was accidentally discovered possible to dive headfirst through the composition partition that separated the ante-room from the dining-room, without suffering much bodily detriment. As Mess President, it was my duty to have the Pioneers up to remove the damaged partitions before the colonel arrived in the morning and, as it was not usually possible to have the replacements fitted in time, it became customary to explain the missing walls by saying that the Mess President was making a few alterations.

'Most peculiar,' the colonel said, after about the third occasion. 'Angus is always altering the Mess, but I can never see any difference.'

Angus Macdonald and I shared a Chinese boy, called Ah Ling, who made absolutely no sense at all and, furthermore, spoke no known language. The first day that we acquired this menial Angus told him to lay out mess-dress for dinner. When we went to change, we found our shotguns on our beds. Angus said that for 'mess-kit' he must have read 'musket', but we never got this point satisfactorily settled.

There was also some doubt as to whether Ah Ling looked after us or we looked after him; so, after a time, we took to fining him and, in this connection, Angus kept an elaborate account. When the first pay-day came round Ah Ling owed us 25 dollars, by Angus's calculations. David Wilson had a much better system with his boy, Ah Tee, which was to deal with all misdemeanours by throwing him out of the window. Ah Tee, who had the consistency and conformity of an india rubber ball, used to accept David's summary awards with good cheer. He stayed with David till the end of the war and never got any better as a servant. A remarkable couple!

One of the assets of Singapore was that you could play almost any game on first-class grounds and there was sailing and flying besides. Quite a few of us were members of the Yacht Club and Angus Macdonald and Michael Blackwood both had boats. A number of the younger officers took up flying, and why none of them ever broke their necks was a mystery to me. There was great rivalry between the Yacht Squadron and the Air Squadron, which took the form of mock battles over the harbour on Saturdays. The Air Squadron, however, were adjudged to have suffered a strategical defeat when they all lost their numbers for dangerous flying on the same afternoon.

Most of us took an active part in the night life of the city, which, apart from Saturdays, closed down sharp at midnight—an excellent institution in many ways. Saturday was the only occasion on which the locals dressed for dinner and, on these nights, it was the established custom to extend the fun and frolic far into the early hours of the morning at the Tanglin Club; having laid a formal foundation during the earlier part of the evening at Raffles' Hotel. Sunday morning was either spent playing golf or sailing, and these sports would culminate in a *curry tiffin,* which was quite the most vicious social pastime that it has ever been my lot to encounter.

The prelude to *tiffin* consisted of anything from one to three hours' drinking and this, on top of the meal itself, was guaranteed to prostrate the toughest constitution. When the *tiffin* was finished, everyone took to the privacy of their own bedrooms and this well-established tradition was known as 'lying-off'. I used to make it a point of honour to play a round of golf after these orgies but it was frequently a most painful experience.

Apart from the orthodox European social activities, I participated in a few Asiatic entertainments. The best of these was a dance given by some Malay ratings, who, I thought, employed an interesting technique. *Les Girls* consisted of a small specially selected team. Having mounted a stage, they assumed expressions of formal animation and then initiated a quiet but rhythmic movement to a guitar accompaniment. Subsequently, *Les Beaux,* according to how the spirit moved them, would assault the platform and dance to their selected girls with the utmost dash and abandon. There was, apparently, only one rule, which was that you were not allowed to touch. The idea was to try and get your girl friend moving in double time. If you couldn't achieve this, which invariably seemed to be the case, you gave way to the *next gallant,* and so the fun went on.

The only Chinese entertainment which I attended was a play. The chief features of this were that the scene-shifting was carried out during acts and that the play continued for five hours after I had left, to the entire satisfaction of the audience. Minor features were that the leading man got so drunk that he couldn't leave the stage and that nobody in the audience had the slightest idea what the play was about anyhow.

I also went to a Japanese dinner party in a restaurant. The party consisted of some of my brother officers, and we were given a small private room which contained no furniture except for an 18-inch-high circular table, with a hole in the centre, round which we sat, tailor-fashion. The floor was spotlessly clean and boots had to be removed on the threshold, but, to add the necessary character to the room, a small vomitorium was attached. The procedure was very correct and, after a few rounds of rice wine, an old woman came in with a charcoal burner and a frying-pan which she positioned in the centre of the table before starting to cook.

It was no ordinary cooking either, and the ingredients were added in the following order: lashings of butter, bamboo shoots and other vegetables, slabs of chicken, a quantity of raw eggs and some soya-bean sauce. After dinner, which was theoretically eaten with chopsticks, in came the *Geisha* girls. You had to order these beforehand, and we contracted for a brace. These *Geishas* are professional entertainers and, in the better class establishments, definitely not prostitutes. The singing and dancing is very quiet and formal and what strikes me now, looking back on it all, is that Jap dancing and Jap tactics have one characteristic in common—they're both done to a pattern. Both are exact and there is no individuality.

Life in Singapore was pleasant enough and there was never a dull moment between work, play and sleep. All the same, a number of us realised that we were living in a fools' paradise, by enforced circumstances, and that the sooner the Press and the Government started to educate the masses for what was coming to them, so much the better. I was, therefore, very pleased when I received orders to sail for India at the beginning of January. Before the war I had obtained a competition vacancy at the Quetta Staff College, as a result of some considerable labour, and now I was to go there on the first war course.

I fondly imagined that, at the end of this course, I would go to the Middle East or Home and, as both of these destinations seemed to offer better prospects of active service than existed in Malaya, I left in great glee, to the accompaniment of some pretty hotly contested parties. The last of these was held by courtesy of the captain, on board the good ship *Suisang,* in which I was due to sail. The vessel turned out to be of such modest displacement that it was only just possible to crush in the whole assembled company. The undoubted success of the party I attributed largely to the high density of guests per square foot. Under these conditions, it is simplicity itself to rid oneself of a bore, whereas, in the more dispersed parties, it is not always possible to do so without giving offence. The lesson is, therefore, to avoid dispersion at parties like the plague. I just mention this, because I find the principle so often violated.

The ship did not sail till the following afternoon and, after a farewell luncheon at the Tanglin Club, David Wilson, who had taken over from me as Transport Officer, did me the signal honour of driving me to the docks in a Bren gun carrier. This created a very deep impression on the master of the *Suisang* and, I think, was one of the reasons which influenced him to allow me to steer his ship, when there were no obstacles within the horizon. There were only two other passengers on board. One was a young American who was going round the world on a motorcycle, which he kept in the hold, and the other was a middle-aged Indian nurse who was returning from a private case in Singapore.

The trip took just over a week, and I spent the time either mastering the rudiments of navigation or lazing in the sun to the accompaniment of some lengthy dissertations on the part of motor-cyclist James E. Lauder, Junior. After a farewell beat up in Calcutta, I found I had a week in hand before the Staff College Course started, so I stepped off at Delhi and availed myself of an open invitation to stay with a brother officer and his wife.

Delhi at Christmas time is quite delightful with its sharp, starlit nights and its warm, cloudless days. I thoroughly enjoyed the variety of brisk entertainments staged on my behalf, which included most kinds of outdoor and indoor sports. I was also glad to have this opportunity of seeing Lutyens's New Delhi for the first, but not by any means the last, time. Apart from its magnificence and splendour, it is, to me, the one and only breath of purity amidst a mass of architectural squalor stretching from the Mediterranean to the Pacific. I liked old Delhi also, although the atmosphere was quite different, and I think Delhi is to India very much what London is to the provinces.

At Quetta, it was bitterly cold and snow was lying on the ground, but I found this very invigorating after the heat and humidity of Malaya. My wife, Alison, was due to come out from England to join me, so I started to set up house on her behalf. In this connection, I was ably assisted by a charming neighbouring wife who had the good sense to see that, as I was quite incapable of striking any of the right notes myself, it would be much better for her to relieve me of all responsibilities. This enabled me to devote a certain amount of time to renewing old friendships and making new ones.

There were sixty-odd officers on the course, all about the same age, of whom rather more than half were married. It was rather like being back at school, but with limitless privileges and none of the disadvantages. We worked pretty hard, but there was time for play also. I acquired a very useful troop horse from the Guides' Cavalry, which bore me well in the hunting field and which I also steered to victory in the Staff College race at the point-to-point. Being the only infantryman in the race 'Charlie' and I started at long odds. In fact, I think Alison was the only one to finance the Tote on our behalf. However, this turned out to be a fine commercial proposition and enabled us to stage a fitting celebration.

Almost overnight winter's bareness was vested in a blaze of multicoloured blossoms on orchard, avenue and lawn, and the snow-capped hills acquired a sparkling gaiety. The *Kohjak* wind blew itself out. Sheepskin coats and fur-lined boots went back into the camphorwood boxes and laughter was heard in the syndicate rooms. And then the blow fell. First Norway, then Holland, Belgium, Dunkirk, St. Valery, and France. Posting instructions arrived and I was ordered to go back to Malaya. It was sad to say goodbye to the many friends one had made, under these catastrophic circumstances—Cables arrived like tradesmen's bills. My eldest brother, Rhoddy, Adjutant of the 1st Highland Light Infantry, was safely back from Dunkirk—my youngest brother, Neil, a soldier in the French Foreign Legion, was missing—

the children, were to be sent to Canada—Rhoddy had received an immediate award of the M.C.—the children could not go to Canada, on account of the dollar exchange. And so, it went on whilst the nails were hammered into the crates, and the *Kahbari Wallahs* brought up the old junk and the servants stood around in shoals waiting for their chits.

Eventually, at the very height of the hot weather, Alison and I caught the afternoon train for Calcutta. Two nights and two more days we spent in that dust-laden carriage, whilst the fans whirled incessantly and the recurrent blocks of ice melted to overflow the bin and form stagnant pools on the unswept floor. I reckon a train journey across India in the hot weather is the highest test of conjugal relations and I recommend anyone to try it out on his *fiancée* if he feels himself in any doubt—providing of course he has the chance.

I fancy there are a number of places which may lay a claim to the title of 'The Midden of the Orient' but personally I back Calcutta against all others; with the possible exception of Rangoon. We had four or five days to wait for our ship and were not sorry when we eventually found ourselves navigating Hoogli Point in a monsoon gale.

On this trip, there were quite a number of passengers on board, including four British officers and their wives; an American professor of the Rockefeller Institute, together with his White Russian wife; also a pianist from a dance band, who was in a half section with a crooning glamour girl; and three or four American oil boys. The oil boys were in a shocking state of health, due to a complete lack of exercise and a surfeit of alcohol. For the most part they stuck to an entirely liquid diet which is not calculated to improve the figure. The White Russian was passionately devoted to Mah-Jong, which game Alison and I learned and, altogether, it was rather a peculiar passenger list.

The other British officers and their wives were a bit insular to start with but, on the 4th of July, the American Colony invited us all to dine as their guests. After an excellent dinner, the health of the President was proposed and this was followed by further speeches, from both guests and hosts, of a goodwill nature, finishing with an international vocal contest. By this time a number of the oil boys had discovered that they possessed a latent talent for crooning and the glamour girl was imparting instruction to the majority of those that were not brushing up their Russian. I gave an impersonation of the Port Doctor carrying out a medical inspection in the first-class saloon,

ANGUS AND ALISON ROSE

and the First Officer gave an ineffective demonstration of how to throw glasses against the wall without breaking them.

When I awoke next morning, I found that we lay anchored in the turbulent waters of the Irrawaddy off Rangoon, and that the captain wanted to see me on the bridge. He had received a signal to say that 'Wife of Captain Rose may *not* repeat *not* accompany him to Singapore'. Pondering this on the promenade deck I ordered a passing steward to bring me a glass of prussic acid and a revolver. Judging my state to a nicety he shortly reappeared with a large 'horse's neck'. I took this with such good effect that the ill-styled instruction soon found itself flowing downstream into oblivion and, a few days later, Alison and I found ourselves steaming through the narrow channel between Blakang Mati and Singapore, under the very shadow of the fortress guns. The luxuriant green hills dipped to the clear, blue water's edge, within a stone's-throw to either side—a picturesque setting but marred by the physical discomfort induced from an overpowering humidity and the ferocity of a tropical sun.

MALAY PENINSULA
AND PART OF EAST INDIES.

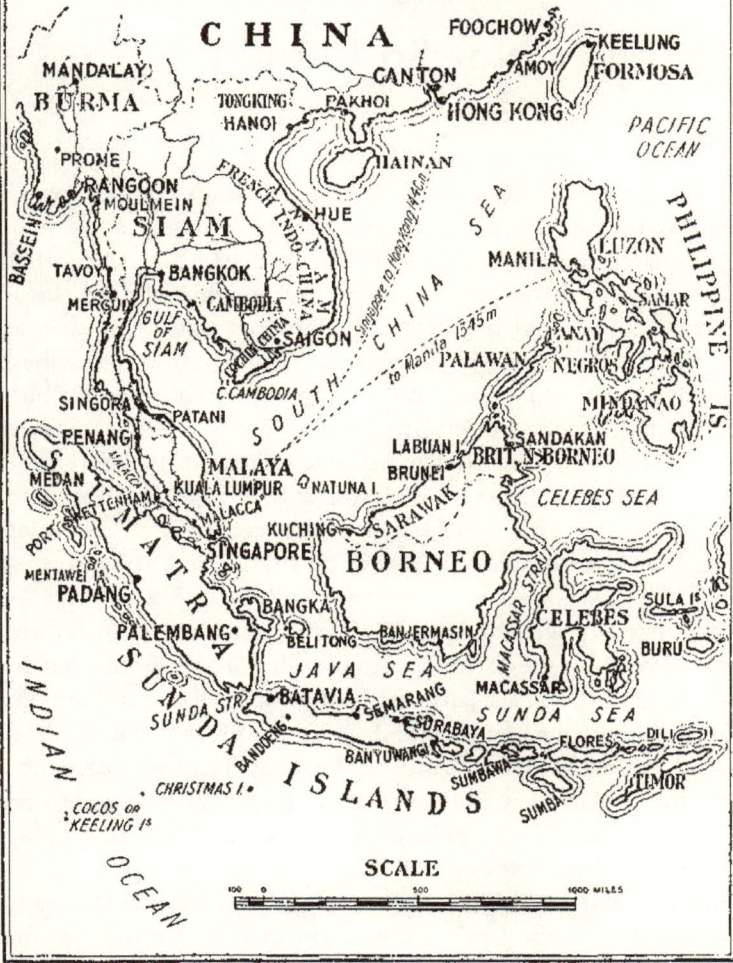

CHINA

FOOCHOW

KEELUNG
FORMOSA

MANDALAY
BURMA

CANTON
AMOY

HONG KONG

TONGKING
HANOI

PAKHOI

PACIFIC
OCEAN

PROME
RANGOON
MOULMEIN
SIAM

HAINAN

HUE

TAVOY
BANGKOK
MERGUI
CAMBODIA
GULF
OF
SIAM

FRENCH INDO-CHINA

SAIGON
C.CAMBODIA

MANILA

LUZON

SAMAR

ANAM

NEGROS

PALAWAN

SOUTH CHINA SEA

Singapore to Hong Kong 1440 m

to Manila 1545 m

PHILIPPINE IS

MINDANAO

SINGORA
PENANG
PATANI

MEDAN

MALAYA
KUALA LUMPUR

PORT SWETTENHAM
SUMATRA
MALACCA

MENTAWEI IS
PADANG

SINGAPORE

NATUNA I.

KUCHING
SARAWAK

LABUAN I.
BRUNEI

BRIT. N.BORNEO

SANDAKAN

CELEBES SEA

BORNEO

SULA IS

BANGKA
PALEMBANG
BELITONG

BANJERMASIN

CELEBES
BURU

JAVA SEA

MACASSAR STRAIT

MACASSAR
SUNDA SEA

INDIAN

SUNDA STR.
BATAVIA
SEMARANG
SOERABAYA

BANDONG
BANYUWANGI

DILI
FLORES
TIMOR

CHRISTMAS I.

SUNDA ISLANDS

SUMBAWA
SUMBA

COCOS OR
KEELING IS

OCEAN

SCALE

100   0   500   1000 MILES

CHAPTER 2

Not So Phoney

After the capitulation of France, French Indo-China soon fell a victim to the Jap aggressor and this had far-reaching consequences on the defence of Malaya. Hitherto Hainan Island had been Japan's furthest advanced base for an attack on the peninsula and the scale of attack was limited by the fifteen hundred odd miles that separated Hainan from Singapore. Now, not only had the Japs established themselves nearly one thousand miles nearer their objective but, by over-running Thailand or violating the neutrality of that country, they would be able to make a land-based attack across the northern frontier of Malaya. Moreover, by virtue of shorter lines of sea communication, the scale of attack was increased and these communications were no longer menaced to the same extent by the United States fortress at Manila.

The first indication the Japs gave of an intended advance through Thailand came in the form of a frontier dispute between French In-do-China and the Thais. Japan stepped in as mediator and settled the difference in favour of Thailand. It was obvious that she would now demand reciprocal favours. Anti-espionage in Thailand was conducted on totalitarian lines, but there seems no doubt that Japan started, forthwith, to build up a military organisation in Thailand, employing the German plain-clothes methods.

In the summer of 1940 Malaya hung like a ripe plum, ready to be knocked off at the Japs' pleasure. Army and R.A.F. reinforcements started to arrive in November 1940 and continued to trickle in during the succeeding months.

The defence was now extended from a purely local one, covering Singapore and the Mersing beaches, to an extensive plan including the whole peninsula and, under the direction of G.H.Q. Far East (Sir

Robert Brooke-Popham), this scheme was part of an even wider policy which embraced the defence of the whole of our territories in the S.W. Pacific; that is to say Malaya, British North Borneo and Sarawak, Burma, Hong Kong and poor little Christmas Island.

As far as Malaya was concerned the policy of the defence was that the peninsula would be held by the R.A.F. Accordingly, aerodromes were constructed over the length and breadth of the country. Troops would, of course, be necessary for the protection of these aerodromes and the actual military dispositions were made with this end in view.

The detail of our dispositions had to conform to the possible courses of attack open to the enemy since the Jap, being the aggressor, had the inherent advantage of the initiative. There were three main courses open to the Jap. He might employ any or all of these courses and we had to be prepared for the worst circumstances. In the first place, he might make a direct sea-borne attack on Singapore. Secondly, he might effect landings on the east coast and advance overland to Johore. Thirdly, he might attack from across the Thai border and advance down the peninsula to Johore. Once he had established himself on the toe of the mainland, overlooking the Johore Straits, the Naval Base would be automatically neutralised and the culmination of the campaign would be an assault on the island.

The military reinforcements, which arrived during 1940 and 1941, consisted of the 11th and 9th Indian Divisions, which were formed into 3rd Indian Corps, and the 8th Australian Division (referred to afterwards as the A.I.F.). In addition, the two British battalions which were evacuated from Shanghai must be added to the troops detailed in the first chapter. The ack-ack defences were also reinforced but, apart from ancillary troops, this was the sum total of our military assets. The strength of the R.A.F., when the Japs arrived, consisted, to the best of my knowledge, of barely 150 aircraft: and what aircraft! There were three or four Brewster-Buffalo fighter squadrons and one Blenheim fighter squadron. The Buffaloes were very inferior machines and, apart from being unmanoeuvrable, their guns gave a lot of trouble.

On the bomber side, there were three Blenheim squadrons, two Wildebeeste torpedo squadrons and one Hudson squadron. The Wildebeestes were relics of another age and two of the Blenheim squadrons were the out-of-date short-nosed variety.

With these Air Force and Army contingents we had to make suitable dispositions to meet the three main courses open to the Japs. For the defence of Northern Malaya, against a land-based attack across the

Thai frontier, 3rd Corps (Lieut.-General Sir Lewis Heath) disposed 11th Indian Division (Major-General Murray Lyon). The aerodromes for the defence of Northern Malaya were sited at Alor Star, Sungei Patani, Butterworth, Penang and then in depth through Taiping, Ipoh and Kuala Lumpur. As far as the east coast was concerned, it was our policy only to defend those areas where possible landing places gave direct access to the main inland communications, as it was obviously impossible to dispose troops along the whole of this enormous coastline. An examination of the map shows these places to be Kota Bahru, Kuantuan, and our old friend Mersing. 3rd Corps disposed the two brigades of 9th Indian Division (Major-General Barstow) on the beaches of Kota Bahru and Kuantuan, whilst the defence of the Mersing beaches and the inland communications of Johore were the responsibility of the two brigades in Major-General Gordon Bennett's Australian Division. Aerodromes, with satellites, existed at Kota Bahru and Kuantuan, and also at Kluang, in Johore, but there was none at Mersing.

Singapore Fortress was commanded by Major-General Keith Simmons. Apart from Fortress troops, there was a mobile garrison of two infantry brigades, which was just about sufficient to hold the open beaches from the western outskirts of the town to Changi. In Singapore, there were aerodromes at Sembawang, Seletar, Kallang, and Tengah.

3rd Indian Corps, the A.I.F., and Singapore Fortress were under Malaya Command H.Q. and the only Command reserve consisted of 12th Indian Infantry Brigade (Brigadier Paris). Lieut.-General Percival had replaced General Bond as G.O.C. in C., in the early months of 1941, and he knew a good deal about the strategy of Singapore as he had previously held the appointment of General Staff Officer 1st Grade when Malaya Command was in its teething stages.

The R.A.F. and Army Commands were amalgamated into a combined H.Q. with a joint planning room, but at the same time the R.A.F., under Air Vice-Marshal Pulford, was controlled by G.H.Q. Far East so that the characteristic of strategic mobility, inherent to the air arm, might be exploited to the full.

An examination of this strategic layout indicated quite clearly to me that, if we did not achieve and maintain air superiority, we were bound to lose Malaya and Singapore in the end because, once the R.A.F. was dominated, the Japs would have complete freedom of manoeuvre at sea and this would pin down our detachments at Kota

Bahru, Kuantuan, Mersing and Singapore. We therefore stood to be defeated in detail, unless we could form a sufficiently large mobile reserve, or mass of manoeuvre. To form any such reserve was quite out of the question, as there were already insufficient troops for the tasks in hand. The very best provision that could be made was in the shape of 12th Indian Infantry Brigade, which was a totally inadequate force for the purpose. On top of this there were no local reserves to replace tired or battle-worn troops and it stood to reason, therefore, that we either had to win the initial battles on each and every front or else lose the war.

Our position seemed desperate except for the fact that the R.A.F. assured us that, such was the superiority of shore-based aircraft against seaborne attack, the enemy would be reduced to complete impotency by the tune our troops were called upon to come into action; or, in other words that the individual weakness of our various military detachments must be regarded in the light of the strength conferred upon the whole defensive layout by our Air Force. In this connection, we were, of course, banking on complete air superiority.

We did, however, grossly underestimate the potential strength of the Jap air arm. It was held that their pilots were as blind as bats and couldn't hit a thing, and not only were we surprised by the efficiency of their pattern bombing high-level attacks, which devastated our aerodromes, but the superiority of the Jap Navy Zero fighter over our Brewster-Buffaloes also came as a heavy shock and a rude awakener to our complacency. Even so, in spite of these material and tactical surprises, I fail to see how anyone, in their wildest moments of optimism, could derive any comfort whatsoever from the types and figures of aircraft which were available. On top of this the majority of the pilots were still only partially trained and the wastage of aircraft in flying accidents was high. The stiffening of experienced pilots was meagre and I doubt if there were a dozen who had experienced actual fighting in the Middle East or Britain.

When I arrived back from the Staff College there was grave anxiety over a Jap invasion. I took over D Company immediately and acquainted myself with the scheme for rounding up Japanese aliens. By day we were at two hours' notice for this task, but at immediate call by night.

Training in the battalion went on apace. I covered a lot of ground with my company and gained an intimate knowledge of the whole of the western part of the island which was to stand me in good stead

GULF OF THAILAND

COCHIN CHINA

Victoria Point

THAILAND

SOUTH CHINA SEA

XX 5(-)

XXXX TWENTY FIFTH YAMASHITA

Singora

8 Dec

Patani

10 Dec

Yala

56(+) 18 (TAKUMI DET)

11-12 Dec Jitra

Alor Star

Gurun

Sik

14-15 Dec Sungei Patani

16-17 Dec

Kroh

Grik

Kuala Krai

13-14 Dec

Kota Bharu

19 Dec

Georgetown Butterworth

PENANG IS.

MALAYA

Bertram

Kuala Trengganu

Kuala Dungun

Kerteh

Kuala Kangsar

24 Dec

Ipoh

Merapoh

23 Dec

British withdrew without pressure to Jerantut and Gemas.

Lumut

Kampar

30 Dec-3 Jan

Bidor

Kuala Lipis

Jerantut

1-3 Jan

Kuantan

1-2 Jan

Telok Anson

Sabak

Trolak

Romb

7 Jan

7 Jan

Kuala Kubu

Maran

Pekan

Pahong

Kuala Selangor

Kuala Lumpur

Karak

Kuala Lipis

55 (-)

Port Swettenham

11 Jan

Seremban

Bahau

14 Jan

Endau

Mersing

Port Dickson

Gemas

JOHORE

Jemaluang

XX GUARDS

Malacca

15-16 Dec

Muar

24-25 Jan

Kluang

STRAIT OF MALACCA

SUMATRA

Johore Bahru

British forces closed on Singapore Island 31 January.

Singapore

LEGEND

Principal road : all weather

Principal road : seasonal

MALAYA, 1941: TOPOGRAPHY

JAPANESE CENTRIFUGAL OFFENSIVE, DECEMBER 1941- JANUARY 1942

Twenty Fifth Army Operations in Malaya

ELEVATIONS IN METERS
0   500   1000   OVER

0   50   100

SCALE IN NAUTICAL MILES APPROX.

⊙ British Airfields

⊙ Japanese Airfields in Thailand

when we were fighting the Japs over the same ground some eighteen months later. I tried to develop original ideas for keeping the men interested in training and, although I had most of the battalion roughs in my company, we were rapidly becoming a high-quality sub-unit.

Our strategical position continued to deteriorate and every Saturday I used to talk to my company on Imperial strategy, so that the men could appreciate the vital but unspectacular role that they were fulfilling in Singapore. These talks also prepared them for the succession of military reverses which I expected would be sprung upon us, and the evacuation of Somaliland in August was no surprise to D Company.

I was particularly anxious as to the fate of our little Somaliland Expeditionary Force as I knew my younger brother in the Black Watch was serving there with his regiment. A few days after the evacuation I had a cable from my mother to say he was wounded but safe, and a further cable arrived to say he had received the immediate award of a D.S.O. for leading a successful counter-attack and driving the Italians back at the point of the bayonet.

After six weeks of regimental soldiering, at the beginning of September, I was appointed Staff Captain in the Quartermaster-General's Branch of Malaya Command, by virtue of my Staff College qualifications. This 'Q' job was not at all to my liking. I sat surrounded by files from early morning till late at night. Most of the work could have been done by an experienced and intelligent clerk, well versed in procedure and regulations. The trouble is, though, that with the expansion of our peace-time army sufficient trained clerks can never be found to meet all the requirements and the consequence is that officers, who should be commanding troops, are employed as ineffective substitutes. I took very badly to the exchange of my commander's sword for a clerk's pen and, although I did achieve some constructive work, in spite of the customary intransigence of the Financial Adviser, I was not sorry to be offered promotion and upgrading some three months later in the capacity of Brigade Major, Penang Fortress.

Of two things accomplished the first was to get War Office sanction for an increased scale of clothing for the troops. The existing scale was totally inadequate but the soldiers made up their deficiencies by purchasing the extra items from their monthly clothing allowance. On the war system of accounting, clothing allowance is suspended and, consequently, the men now had to make up their requirements from their own money. The whole principle was wrong and I was pleased when I got this injustice rectified. My second achievement was to obtain authority for an adequate scale of liquid prismatic compasses to be included in the Unit War Equipment Tables. Cross-country movement through jungle was entirely dependent on oil compasses and we were still working on the scale considered necessary in the trenches of the last war. These compasses took two years to arrive but one of them I used, personally, in the subsequent campaign.

Towards the end of December Alison and I packed up and moved to Penang. When I arrived there, I found that it was a fortress in name only. There were two out-of-date batteries of 6-inch guns and the mobile garrison consisted of one Indian Infantry battalion and one battalion of Straits Settlements Volunteers; but the latter were not very mobile. In addition to this we had a Fortress Company of Sappers and a labour battalion.

I was responsible for the defence plan of the island and this included the siting and construction of beach defences and obstacles, the defence of the aerodrome against paratroop attack and of vulnerable points against sabotage. I was also responsible for security and intelligence. The work was quite interesting and, although we never had anything like sufficient troops to defend the island, I drew up a masterly scheme which catered for anything from one to five battalions being allotted to the Fortress commander.

Penang was, in reality, a satellite fortress in relation to Singapore. There was a possibility that the Japs, instead of carrying out a direct sea-borne attack on Singapore or landing on the eastern coast, might sail their fleet through the Sunda Straits and then up the west coast of Sumatra, with the object of taking Penang as a base for further operations against Singapore. However, once they were in a position to deliver a land-based attack from Thailand the strategic significance of Penang entirely went by the board. It retained a certain tactical significance on account of its aerodrome, but that was all.

When the war came Penang never fired a shot for the simple reason that it was not geographically placed to stop an enemy advance on the mainland. The Indian battalion was dispatched to fight under 11th Division, the volunteers disintegrated, and the fortress troops were left to take over the running of the entire essential services, which completely broke down under the weight of the heavy Japanese unopposed air attacks. There was no ack-ack defence in Penang because the equipment had not arrived out from home. A good deal of mud has been slung by ill-informed persons about the evacuation of Penang but the Jap was quick to see that an attack on this virtually undefended fortress would provide him with a strong political weapon which he could turn to good account in the propaganda field.

The fortress was commanded by Brigadier Lyon. He had been originally commissioned at the time of the Boer War and was called back from retirement to take up this appointment, on account of his qualifications as an experienced fortress gunner. 'Tiger' Lyon was a keen sportsman and had been a fine all-round athlete in his day. He was an excellent commander to work under and he decentralised all details to the Staff Captain and myself, merely directing us on matters of policy. 'Tiger' and I became close friends and it used to give him great pleasure whenever I succeeded in running up a respectable score in the local cricket matches. I used to play cricket on Sundays and also in the occasional two-day Inter-State matches. These contests were great fun and I enjoyed them not only for the cricket but also for the entertainment and good fellowship that went with them.

Malcolm Moffat was the Staff Captain. He had served in the last war and then left the army and gone into business. Most of his career had been spent in Malaya and his knowledge of the country was invaluable to him in his present job. He was a born soldier and an outstandingly efficient officer. 'Tiger', Malcolm and I all got on very well together and it was a happy and cheerful headquarters.

After nine months of a most pleasant existence in Penang, I was offered the job of General Staff Officer 2nd Grade (Training) in Malaya Command. As training was the aspect of soldiering that interested me most and as Penang really was rather a backwater, I decided to accept the offer of this appointment; so, in September, Alison and I packed up our house yet another time and moved back to Singapore.

Alison was expecting a baby in the near future so we did not set up house till after the event as the Millers had very kindly asked us to stay with them. David Miller was 'Number One' of the Chartered Bank in Penang and had recently been moved to Singapore. He and I used to partner each other in the four-ball matches which were such a feature of the Royal Singapore Golf Club. One day when I was playing rather below form and we were several balls down David suggested that I would do better with a new set of clubs. In view of the fact that he was my bank manager I did not let this opportunity slip and cashed in on a set of Henry Cotton's the following day. Poor David contracted enteric fever during his evacuation from Singapore and died shortly after reaching Ceylon This was a tragic blow, particularly for his charming and vivacious wife, Gwen, and their two children.

On Hallowe'en Alison gave birth to a sizable girl, without turning a hair, and this put the score up to three as we already had a boy and a girl at home. We then took up residence in a comfortable house amidst pleasant surroundings, near the golf club, and here we lived a flat-out existence consisting of work and entertainment.

Malaya Command had grown out of all recognition since my departure the previous Christmas. Most of the original staff had gone up a rank or two and there were more red hats about. As a member of the 'Chairborne Division' I had one of the better jobs which necessitated touring round the country and watching the various exercises and manoeuvres I then had the duty of writing up accounts of the battles and drawing the correct lessons and deductions from what I had seen. These would go up to the G.O.C. through the medium of my G.S.O.I and the Brigadier General Staff, and be returned with suitable comments. From this data, I used to draft the Command Training Instructions and, since I had been the victim of heavy military phraseology for so long as a regimental officer I did my best to ease the lot of my potential public. However, I fear that my style was sometimes considered too flighty to be laid before the general and this would entail a re-draft.

I enjoyed thoroughly this part of my work as the daytime could be spent in the field with troops and the writing could be dealt with after dark in my own study. However, I had a host of less interesting duties which held me pinned to the office desk. These included the distribution of vacancies at Command and Indian Army Schools, the provision of ranges, the supervision of Passive Air Defence and the distribution of manuals. I had two G.S.O.3s who stood me in good stead and did their best to cope with the rising tide which flooded my 'In' basket as soon as I left the office.

Returning from a three-day exercise on one occasion, 'Pluto' Gordon, who was my minion for Chemical Warfare, informed me that we were in bad odour on account of having ordered respirators for the civilians. There had been a small mistake over this. I had initiated a proposal for equipping the civilian employees in the H.Q. with respirators, as I considered that it would be unbecoming for an officer and a gentleman to permit some of the better-looking girls in the building to succumb to poison fumes, without making a gesture in the style of Sir Philip Sidney. I had therefore instructed 'Pluto' to order respirators for the civilians and he had quite understandably ordered them for all the civilians in Malaya, as they had none and there had been a lot of controversy over this question.

Personally, I thought 'Pluto' had not done too badly, but I was officially informed that a different view was taken by the authorities. On the opposite side of the building in the 'Q' branch of the staff I was fortunate enough to have Desmond Sheane as a brother staff officer. Desmond and I had been at the Staff College together, where we had become close friends, and his quick wit and originality did much to relieve the monotony of office routine. Apart from providing a continual source of entertainment he was an outstandingly efficient officer and a loss to the Service when he had the ill-fortune to be amongst those taken when Singapore fell.

CHAPTER 3

The Deluge

By the end of November, the crisis was upon us. On the afternoon of Saturday November 29th, I had just holed out on the ninth green when I noticed an R. A. F. orderly leaving the club house, carrying a signaller's satchel. On returning to the club house at the end of the round, we heard that the troops had been put at 'Second Degree of Readiness'. This entailed moving to battle stations and manning all defences and headquarters in skeleton. This was not the first time we had been put at 'Second Degree of Readiness' and these scares invariably happened either on Saturdays or over Easter and other festivities

Alison and I were flinging a party that night, in celebration of her release from *purdah*, and everyone rang up to find out if it was still on. I said it would certainly be on, and all and sundry who were not on duty duly turned up. We had a buffet supper in our house and then went on to dance at the Tanglin Club. With many elegant girls and handsome officers, we contrived quite a 'Duchess of Richmond's Ball' atmosphere and so it turned out that this was the last evening on which we danced and gallivanted together.

During the course of the next week the situation continued to deteriorate. On the Sunday I went up to Malacca to watch my own battalion training on the newly acquired field firing range. The Jocks were in very high spirits and spoiling for a fight.

On Saturday morning, a large fleet of Japanese transports, heavily escorted, was sighted off Cape Cambodia by our Catalina aircraft. They were steaming north-west into the Gulf of Thailand. This was the signal for putting troops at 'First Degree of Readiness' and, after lunch, I was rung up by a staff officer and told to report for duty in the Operations Room at 4 p.m.

The Operations Room at Malaya Command was shared by the

Army and Air Force Staffs. It was a large wooden hut 112 feet long and 40 feet wide. The walls were plastered with maps and charts. There were more maps and charts on long tables and the place was one mass of telephones. Surrounding the Ops. Room there were dozens of similar huts for Signals, Intelligence Staffs and also for the accommodation of officers and clerks. This headquarters was at Sime Road, next door to the Royal Singapore Golf Club, and it constituted a camp of its own.

There was nothing to do at all during my first tour of duty, which finished at midnight on Saturday, but I employed myself, usefully, by making myself conversant with the R.A.F. Staff organisation, maps and aircraft availability charts.

We had no further news about the Jap fleet the next morning, as they were out of range of our Catalina aircraft by this time. There was a lot of conjecture as to whether this move, on the part of the Japs, was not all bluff; and the majority of officers who had personal experience of the Japs in China were convinced that there would still be no war. When I came on duty in the War Room, on Sunday at midnight, I was informed that the last light Catalina reconnaissance had reported the Jap fleet steaming due south, parallel to the coast of Thailand, and that they were in a position to arrive off Kota Bahru between 0100 and 0200 hours that Monday morning. One Catalina had failed to return, so it now looked pretty obvious that the Nips were 'coming a' shootin'' that night.

There was one G.S.O.2 always on duty in the War Room. Our job was to be thoroughly in the picture as regards the whole battle situation on all fronts. We took the telephone conversations down from 3rd Corps, the A.I.F. and Singapore Fortress, and from this source and Signals messages we compiled the 'War Diary'. Matters of policy we referred to the B.G.S. or the G.S.O.1, one of whom was always on duty. Once in every tour of duty we used to send situation reports to the War Office with copies to the governor and to India and various other addressees. An eight-hour shift in the War Room was a pretty exhausting duty as it entailed continuous concentration without a break. If you let up for a second you never caught up again and very often there was not even time to eat a sandwich. Alison, used to get so stuffy if I got home without having victualled myself that I usually had to eat my food in the car on the way back.

When I took over at 0001 hours on December 8th, I suggested to the B.G.S. that the code-word 'Black-out' should be dispatched, but he told me that the governor was responsible for ordering the issue of this message and that no action was to be taken in the meantime. It seemed to me that if the situation demanded troops being fully deployed in their battle positions, an equivalent gesture was surely warranted on the part of the house dwellers. However, the governor declined to order 'Blackout' and that was that. No doubt there was some good reason.

I had been on duty for about an hour and a quarter and was engaged in conversation with the R.A.F. operations Staff Officer, when the secraphone, or 'green line' telephone, ejected a sharp peal. The R.A.F. officer grasped the receiver and it soon became apparent that Kota Bahru aerodrome was at the other end of the line. There was a strong suspicion that ships were off the coast. Visibility was very bad and what action was to be taken? The Air Officer Commanding now appeared on the scene and put through a call to G.H.Q., Far East. After a bit more talking, the identity of ships out to sea appeared quite definite.

'Someone's opened fire,' said Kota Bahru.

'Who, us or the Japs?' queried the Ops. officer.

'Us, I think. No, it wasn't—it was the Japs.'

The conversation brought me back to a history lesson at my private school, about Wolfe dying at Quebec. 'They run, sir.' 'Who run;' 'The French run.' 'Then, thank God, I die happy.'

Yes, there appeared to be no doubt that the Japs had opened fire and the thunder of guns could be heard through the telephone. The atmosphere was electric. Air Vice-Marshal Pulford chipped in on the conversation and ordered the Hudson squadron to take off and attack.

War—the war that we had been waiting and training for during the last two years—had started. As I entered the historic event into the War Diary, I pondered as to the result and I confess that I viewed the prospects with little confidence.

The telephone conversation with Kota Bahru continued without interruption. Our aircraft had apparently met with heavy and accurate 'flak' over the Jap fleet. Kota Bahru wanted to know whether they should bomb the cruisers or the transports.

'Go for the transports, you bloody fools,' shouted the Ops officer down the telephone.

'Dear God,' I thought. 'Didn't they even know that.'

Reports kept coming in the whole night about hits and near misses on various craft. Barges, heavily loaded with Japs, were reported to have been sunk in the Kelantan River. Somewhere about 4 a.m. the Singapore ack-ack artillery opened up. I looked at the envelope on the table containing the code message 'Black-out'.

'Put the lights out,' someone shouted.

'Light the hurricane lamps,' added someone else.

"That's bombs,' said Bill Waller, one of the G.S.O.3s, and, after a pause, 'That's ack-ack.'

I learned afterwards, that the Singapore locals, who had no idea that there was a war on, thought that we were indulging in a realistic exercise and the opening salvoes of ack-ack were the signal for everyone to jump out of bed and put on their unblacked-out lights. This must have been of considerable assistance to the Jap raiders. Actually, very few aircraft took part in the attack. I think it amounted to three small formations of about nine to twelve aircraft in each. Seletar and Tengah aerodromes were objectives and bombs were also dropped in the commercial centre of the town.

By first light the R.A.F. reported they had repelled the attack at Kota Bahru and that the few remaining Japs ashore were making their get-away as best they could. The news was excellent and, on the existing information, there appeared no doubt that the day was ours. In fact, the G.O.C. sent a message to Brigadier Key, complimenting him on drawing first blood, but adding that the first round did not necessarily decide the contest. However, even this turned out to be a bit premature as, later in the morning, a report arrived, from Brigadier Key, to say that he had lost the whole of one beach and one or two pill-boxes on another. He said he was going to direct the counter-attack personally and hoped to clear up the situation by the afternoon.

Worse news was to follow. The counter-attacks failed and the Japs were reported to have infiltrated to considerable depth. The R.A.F. reported that the aerodrome was surrounded and they abandoned it in some haste, leaving the whole of their petrol and bomb stores behind. The petrol was destroyed by a gallant gunner officer, named Close, who remained to fight against whatever odds presented themselves. He was subsequently awarded the Military Cross and posted as missing.

The whole story of Kota Bahru can only be written by collating the evidence of the troops that actually took part but there seems little doubt on the following points: First, the Japs suffered very severe casualties at sea from bombing, from the small arms fire and 18-pounders manned by the infantry in the beach defences, and by drowning in the surf. Secondly, only small parties of Jap stalker snipers succeeded in infiltrating, but they did this quickly and most skilfully and exploited to a great depth. Thirdly, our troops reported their own positions and the position of neighbouring units as considerably worse than was actually the case. Conversely, they overestimated the strength of the Jap positions. Rumours and exaggerations were rife, largely due to the troops being inexperienced. Fourthly, the aerodrome was prematurely abandoned.

Read here the moral roundly writ
For him who into battle goes —
Each soul that hitting hard or hit,
Endureth gross or ghostly foes.
Prince, blown by many overthrows,
Half blind with shame, half choked with dirt,
Man cannot tell, but Allah knows
How much the other side was hurt!

Although at first light it seemed as if we had won the first round, the situation by the evening of December 8th was very different. Not only had the Japs secured a firm bridgehead on the Kota Bahru beaches but they had also got the aerodrome and the 8th Indian Infantry Brigade was in retreat. On the morning of December 9th, Brigadier Key was reported to have been captured, together with his headquarters, but this proved to be merely one of those alarmist rumours that were one of the main features of the Malayan Campaign. 8th Brigade's positions appeared to be almost hopeless, at that time, as it was still believed that the Japs were ashore in considerable strength. The 4/19th Hyderabad Regiment, from the 12th Brigade, was dispatched by rail and road to help extricate Brigadier Key's apparently doomed force.

The brigadier, however, succeeded in rallying his units and occupying a rear-guard position at Machang which lay just over half-way between Kota Bahru and his railhead at Krai.

Now that the beaches and the aerodromes were lost, there was no point in retaining the 8th Brigade in its present position and it was, therefore, decided to withdraw this formation to the interior. The only route of withdrawal was down the 120 miles of railway that connected Kula Krai with Kula Lipis. The withdrawal was kept a closely guarded secret from all but the senior staff officers, but this delicate operation was carried out successfully, over a period of days, somewhere about December 18th. Considerable reserves of stores had been accumulated in front of railhead but, I believe, except for a certain amount of transport, most of our equipment was withdrawn intact.

I venture to say that, had the Japs landed in the strength which we supposed they had, this withdrawal would never have materialized. In actual fact, Brigadier Key's rear-guard was never seriously pressed. A captured prisoner reported that all the Jap armour had been sunk at sea, and Richard Dent, who was a friend of mine and Brigade Major to this formation, told me that, in his opinion, not more than six hundred Japs were ashore on the evening of December 8th; against which we had the best part of four battalions still remaining.

Kota Bahru was probably our nearest approach to a victory in Malaya and, had we maintained our positions, the morale effect on the troops as a whole would have been immense. As it was, we developed an inferiority complex at Kota Bahru, and, in the withdrawal to Kula Krai, the 'wind-up' firing at night was so prolific that, eventually, the Brigadier withdrew all ammunition from the troops at night except for one round per weapon. This not only produced a steadying effect, but also reduced night engagements to nil and our own casualties accordingly.

Whilst the withdrawal from Kelantan State was being effected, the enemy remained active on the eastern coast of Malaya. Our R.A.F. reconnaissance only gave the vaguest information of what was happening. There were rumours of enemy landings in the Federated State of Terengganu which were subsequently confirmed. On the night of December 9th-10th a battle took place on the beaches at Kuantuan; but it was never quite certain if the enemy actually participated in this hotly contested action. Wild rumours were flying about in the Mersing area and, here again, wind-up firing was rife. Rumours and counter-rumours went around like wildfire, and these included beach and paratroop landings and fifth column activities.

The Japs were reputed to know every movement of our aircraft from the time they left their hangars to the time they became airborne and I have no doubt that this was true. The aircraft availability chart in the Operations Room made worse reading every hour. Our Brewster-Buffalo fighters had already proved themselves no match for the Jap Zeros and our Blenheim bomber raids were pathetically ineffective, in spite of the individual gallantry of crews. The self-destruction of our own aircraft, in flying accidents, continued at the normal high rate, and the morale of the majority of the ground staffs soon fell to the level one would expect from the standard of discipline that prevailed.

On December 9th, it stood out quite clearly that the R.A.F. had been decisively beaten; but worse was to follow, as December 10th marked the dusk of a night that was to bring forth no dawn. It was on this day that our fine ships, *Prince of Wales* and *Repulse,* were sunk off the east coast of Malaya. As far as I could gather, these ships left Singapore to operate against Japanese convoys off the east coast of Thailand. From hearsay evidence, I was given to understand that the ships had gone some distance up the coast and had then turned back on being spotted by Jap reconnaissance aircraft.

Whilst on the return journey information of a Jap convoy had been received and the ships turned course to attack. Whether or not R.A.F. support was pre-arranged I am unable to say, but there were certainly none of our aircraft on the scene till both ships had gone down. The action began with a high-level bombing attack, followed by devastating low level torpedo attacks. The Jap aircraft, apparently, took no avoiding action and it was quite impossible for the battleships to engage all the aircraft that came in. Both ships avoided something in the nature of sixteen to nineteen torpedoes and were struck by an approximately equal number.

I was on duty in the Operations Room from 4 p.m. to midnight on that day, and my first intimation of the disaster was a pilot's reconnaissance report of a large patch of oil and a destroyer picking up survivors in a certain area off Tioman Island. This message was being taken down by a R.A.F. operational clerk and, as it seemed pretty important, I went across to the Air Officer Commanding and asked him if he had yet received this information. The A.O.C. said, 'What do you know about this;'

'Exactly what I have told you, sir,' I replied.

'Well, don't ask any questions. You'll hear about it later.'

I knew what had happened then, but I didn't know it was both ships. The sinkings were kept a deadly secret from the junior staff officers. Soon afterwards, I was speaking to the commander of 3rd Corps on 'the green line' and General Heath asked me if it was true that our battleships had been sunk. I said, 'Yes, I believe they have, but we are not supposed to know'. A senior staff officer overheard this and I stopped a rocket for talking out of turn.

Later on, Mr. Duff-Cooper, together with panama hat, Brigade of Guards tie and Personal Assistant came into the Operations Room. His Personal Assistant was Robbie Robertson of my own regiment. Robbie had been one of my greatest friends for many years. He told me that Duff-Cooper was releasing him and that he was going back to the regiment; at which he was more than delighted as it was the chief love of his life. Robbie had very definite ideas on the subject of surrender and it was his personal code that no soldier must ever lay down his arms, however desperate the circumstances. I am sure that, unless he was physically overpowered and taken prisoner, both he and his men would fight to the finish. He was presumed killed, commanding the battalion at Slim River on January 7th, and it was fitting that his end and his life's ambition should coincide. Duff-Cooper announced the loss of our ships in the evening news. The disaster had a morale effect on our troops that can well be appreciated.

In subsequent days, it became apparent that the Japanese were pushing troops ashore on the undefended coastline north of Kuantan and that, after a time, this manoeuvre would constitute a threat against the security of 22nd Indian Infantry Brigade's communications from Kuantan to Jerantut. Eventually, 22nd Brigade was 'winkled' out of position by this threat to their flank and rear and, whilst embussing, they were severely handled in a surprise Japanese attack.

Whilst these operations in North-eastern Malaya were under way, the Japs initiated their main offensive against Malaya, across the Thai frontier. A large proportion of the enemy convoy that had been sighted on December 6th put in at Singora and Patani, in Thailand, and only a detachment carried on to Kota Bahru. Singora was about 65 miles from the frontier. There was, in Malaya Command, a projected plan which envisaged an advance in Thailand. Under certain circumstances we were going to take the offensive across the Thai border, but the details of this plan were a secret in which I was no participant. If we did not advance into Thailand, then 11th Division was to meet the Japanese in a defensive position at Jitra, which was some twenty miles south of the frontier.

In the words of the corps commander, there was no sound reason for taking up a position at Jitra, except that it was less bad than any other alternative position. For the most part, the Jitra position consisted of open *padi* fields. The left of the position rested on the sea and the right in the foothills of the jungle. The divisional front was quite fantastic. I think I am right in saying it was about twenty-five miles. In the wet season, there was a natural anti-tank obstacle over most of the front and, in due course, there was to be an artificial one in the dry season. The artificial obstacle was not yet completed but it was still early on in the wet season. The available lines of advance for the Japs, through the Jitra position, consisted of the main road and the railway. Major-General Murray Lyon disposed three brigades of his 11th Division at Jitra. On the right, all inclusive of the road, was 15th Indian Infantry Brigade (Brigadier Garrett) and on the left, was the 6th Indian Infantry Brigade (Brigadier Ley). In reserve was the newly arrived 28th Gurkha Brigade (Brigadier Carpendale).

The whole conception of the Jitra position was tactically unsound. The flanks had been endlessly prolonged to prevent encirclement. In spite of this the flanks were still open but, what was much worse, the width of the position could only be achieved at the complete disregard of depth. Added to this, depth was still further reduced by virtue of the fact that one battalion from each of the two forward brigades, and another from the reserve brigade, were deployed as an outpost screen in front of, but out of touch with the main position, whilst a second battalion of the reserve brigade was employed in an anti-parachute role at Alor Star.

General Murray Lyon was in no way assisted in his task by Malaya Command, as he was expecting to have to implement the Siam invasion and all his transport and signals were laid out accordingly. When Malaya Command eventually called off the projected offensive, Murray Lyon was pushed for time and his troops were already tired, from lack of sleep, before contact had been made.

The Jap did not advance immediately from his Thai bases. This may have been because he wanted a few days for the preparation of his seaborne forces or, alternatively, he may have delayed in order to allow us to come forward across the frontier, in which case I have little doubt that he would have administered the *coup de grace* to 11th Division, in the open fields of Thailand as, by that time, we had virtually no air force left in existence. I recollect one air attack being made against Singora and from this offensive only one of our aircraft returned; the wounded pilot dying in the cockpit before he had been debriefed.

We sent a strong fighting patrol into Thailand on December 8th but after a short and moderately successful engagement, it was beaten back with a loss of several men and a Bren carrier. The Japs were quick to perceive the weakness of our Jitra position. On December 11th, they came charging down the road in light tanks, throwing grenades out of the turrets, and went through our outposts like the proverbial dose of salts. By the time, they had made contact with our main position the Divisional Commander and Brigadier Garrett were cut off with the outposts, the latter being wounded. These two commanders eventually regained the main body; but the outposts had been filleted, and eliminated from the battle, almost without firing a shot.

The Japs then repeated these tactics against the main position which as we have already seen, lacked any depth. They put in a series of heavy attacks on a narrow frontage astride the main road. All their attacks were taken by the two battalions of 15th Brigade, which were disposed in the vicinity of the road. Our troops put up a good fight and repulsed the first two attacks with heavy loss to the Japs. The Leicesters and the Dogra Regiment bore the brunt of the fighting but some well-timed counterattacks were put in by the Gurkhas. In each attack the Japs probably employed a regimental group, supported by light tanks. In their third attack, they succeeded in breaking through and exploited in depth down the main road. The effect of this was that our troops, who were out to the flanks and had taken no part in the battle, were cut off. This was the position on the morning of December 13th.

General Murray Lyon succeeded in rallying the remnants of the 15th Brigade, a fair proportion of 6th Brigade and the majority of 28th Brigade, and took up a position at Gurun some 40 miles farther south. The main feature of the Gurun position was that it contained all the weaknesses of the Jitra position and none of the advantages. The Japs attacked it on about December 15th, with nothing more than strong fighting patrols, and won the battle almost before it had begun. 6th Brigade took a bad knock at this battle and the Japs surprised and destroyed the whole of the brigade staff with the exception of the brigadier who effected a fortunate escape. The fighting value of the formation was, by now, reduced to the 28th Gurkha Brigade, which was on the right and had not been seriously engaged. The division had lost almost the whole of its transport and also a good deal of equipment. The troops were dog-tired and demoralised and 6th and 15th Brigade certainly had no fight left in them till they were rested and re-equipped.

Neither was this all that happened in the State of Kedah. There was another route from Thailand across into Malaya and this crossed the frontier near a place called Kroh. It was assumed that the Japs would follow their usual tactics of advancing on as broad a front as possible and, to meet the Kroh move, 11th Division had already disposed a detachment of two battalions, under Colonel Moorehead. This force, which was known as Krocol, was to advance across the Thai frontier and establish itself on the reputedly impregnable 'ledge' position, some miles across the border. Krocol made lamentably poor progress and was held up for twenty-four hours by a handful of Thai policemen and a dark rainy night. Their casualties were negligible and there is little doubt that the influence of that dear old peace-time, North-West Frontier policy which considers it a 'bad show' to have casualties (because questions get asked in the House if you do) prejudiced the whole operation. Anyhow, to cut a long story short, Krocol was beaten to it for the 'ledge' position by the Japs and they came bounding back at a considerably faster rate than that at which they had gone forward, with the Nipponese hot on their heels.

No sooner did the Japs reach Kroh than they pressed on in pursuit of Krocol with one force and detached a second force to carry out a wider encircling move, *via* Grik and Lenggong, towards Kuala Kangsar. Luckily we received timely information of this move (which had not been anticipated) through the local police. Consequently a small force, consisting of C Company of the Argyll and Sutherland Highlanders, a detachment of R.A.F. armoured cars and No. 1 Malayan Independent Company, was sent up the Grik Road to contact and delay any Japanese advance.

In the meantime, the two remaining battalions of Brigadier Paris's 12th Brigade (the 3rd battalion being in Kelantan, by now) were dispatched to Baling to extricate the ill-fated Krocol. The date of these moves must have been about December 13th. It is interesting to note the Japanese strategy. His main effort was launched down the arterial road and, at the same time, he brought in an encircling attack designed to hit our line of communication behind the Muda River and a deeper encircling attack directed to cut our communications at the Perak River.

On taking over command at Baling, Brigadier Paris made fresh dispositions with such good effect that he planned to regain the initiative with a counter-attack on the 16th; but no sooner had he reached this stage than a liaison officer arrived from 11th Division to say that the Japs had filleted their Gurun positions and that General Murray Lyon was forced to retreat. To conform to this set-back 12th Brigade was ordered to step back on to the Muda River, at Batu Perkaka, to provide right flank protection to 11th Division's withdrawal.

An ugly situation developed at Batu Perkaka on December 16th when Jap stalker snipers succeeded in seizing the bridge in rear of the 5/2nd Punjab Regiment. Colonel Deakin, their commanding officer, happened to be on the spot and he gallantly restored the situation by

ANGUS ROSE AT THE NORTHWEST FRONTIER

means of an immediate counter-attack, launched by himself and his orderly. This enabled the Punjabis to withdraw and, on the following day, the Argylls fought a successful encounter battle at Titi Karangan, in which they slew over 200 Japs for the loss of 10 men.

This battle produced a dramatic incident. The task that the battalion had been given was to deny a specified line till midday and, as the unit was stretched, by necessity, over four miles, the situation did not look too good. The colonel's plan was as aggressive as circumstances permitted. He placed A Company in ambush, astride the road, with B Company concealed to a flank and in advance of the ambush, ready to pounce on the enemy's rear after contact had been made. The signal for 15 Company's attack was to be the 'Advance' sounded on the bugle. Although this attack was calculated to be the best method of defence, it was appreciated that B Company would be overwhelmed eventually, on account of the limitless reserves which the Japs had at their disposal.

It was, therefore, arranged that in the unlikely event of the attack being unnecessary the bugler would sound the 'Stand Fast' and this would be the signal to disengage.

The troops had spent a miserable night in torrential rain and no one felt in much form for a battle. All the same, A Company's ambush was a tremendous success. The two leading Jap companies were caught in close order at point-blank range and annihilated. Then the Jap reserves came into action and the initiative soon passed to the enemy. The colonel judged the moment for the counter-attack to have arrived and, to hearten the men, he told the Pipe Major to strike up. Just as he turned to order Drummer Hardy to sound the 'Advance' a dispatch rider came dashing up the road and handed the colonel a message. It read 'You may withdraw at your discretion'. Hardy had already sounded the regimental call. 'Stop,' barked the colonel, 'sound the "Stand Fast".'

It was a matter of seconds. The Argylls disengaged and their armoured cars struck the usual, quick, Jap follow-up another rude blow, to complete a thoroughly successful engagement.

The 28th Gurkha Brigade now took over rear-guard and the Argylls, followed by the 5/2nd Punjabis, were diverted to relieve Bobby Kennard's sorely pressed C Company on the Grik road. The Argylls arrived on the 19th and fought a highly successful encounter battle at Sumpitan on the same day. C Company, though still a fighting unit, had lost over 50 per cent of their strength and the Sumpitan battle served its purpose as a check on the Japanese advance. On the 20th and 21st the Highlanders had further successes at Lenggong and Kota Tampan and the 5/2nd Punjabis carried on the good work the following day.

At Kota Tampan, the Japs rafted down the Perak River and put a road block in behind the Argylls. Colonel Stewart got his information from an old Chinaman, who arrived with this alarming report at his H.Q. The colonel slipped the Chinaman ten bucks and dispatched his reserve company in motor transport to clear the road. C Company hit the Japs just as they were establishing their road block and knocked them for six. The Japs disintegrated and the Argylls were able to withdraw intact. It was a well-fought engagement. We had practised it time and time again during our training.

These actions enabled 11th Division to withdraw unmolested behind the Perak River by December 23rd. Here they were reorganised and re-equipped to the full extent of our limited resources. Brigadier Paris took over from General Murray Lyon as Divisional Commander. The 6th and 15th Brigades, which had lost very heavily, were amalgamated. The 12th Brigade was transferred from Command reserve to form an integral part of 11th Division and the 28th Gurkha Brigade completed the division to establishment. Apart from those changes, Brigadiers Garrett and Carpendale were replaced, and Brigadier Ley was already incapacitated from an injury. The new brigadiers were Lieut.-Colonel Stewart, 12th Brigade, and Lieut.-Colonels Moorehead and Selby, 6/15th and 28th Brigades, respectively. Although the bowler-hats had been taken by the commanders in 11th Division, the responsibility for the Jitra debacle and the subsequent repercussions seem to me to fall on Malaya Command. Jitra was, after all, laid-out with the approval of Malaya Command and there is no doubt that the basic conception of the position was tactically unsound.

It is easy to be wise after the event, but our correct tactics should have been to fight from all round defended localities placed astride the main axis of communication and not from a thinly defended line. The latter type of defence was vulnerable to encirclement and filleting, and, moreover, gave no scope for counter-manoeuvre and offensive action.

An alternative plan, offering greater prospects of success, would have been to dispose two of the three brigades astride the main road and railway, in a series of battalion hedgehogs, each with its own mobile reserve for offensive action and each containing at least thirty

At the Northwest Frontier

days' reserves in ammunition and supplies. Behind this defended belt the other brigade should have been kept well to the rear with a role of counterattacking any Japanese encirclement that succeeded in establishing itself on the road in rear of our defensive layout. Out in front, and to the flank of the foremost defended localities, we should have established at least one battalion from the forward brigade, in jungle hideouts, well clear of the main axis.

These hideouts would be in the form of company localities and each company would require one or two alternative positions, all fully stocked with reserves. The role of these units would be to operate offensively against the Japanese line of communications, once contact had been made, and to upset his preparations for overcoming our main defence system. Companies would regard their hideouts as jungle sanctuaries to be used for rest and recuperation between offensive sorties and, once the Japs succeeded in locating and preparing an attack on any one particular hideout, the unit would fade out and move to an alternative position.

A defence of this nature would have been a hard nut to crack, but I don't think it would have prevented Singapore from falling in the end, because any defensive operation is merely a means of giving time for a commander to bring up his mass of manoeuvre for the counterstroke. In Malaya, we had no such element, only poor little 12th Brigade against a potential Jap force of from five to six divisions. With this numerical inferiority, we could never hope to gain the strategic initiative and the Japs would have been able to reduce our defences in time or to bypass them by exploiting their command of the sea; more especially as they now possessed unchallenged air superiority.

To sum up, I think it is fair to say that a correct application of tactics would have enabled us to hold the Japs at the frontier for a matter of days or perhaps even weeks, whereas, in actual fact, we only checked them for a few hours. The point that is of interest is, how would this delay have affected the subsequent Jap break through to the South-West Pacific on the one hand and the frontiers of India on the other. This is a question on which I am insufficiently informed to suggest the answer.

CHAPTER 4

West Coast Raiders

During the odd ten days that I spent in the War Room I got a good knowledge of the fighting in general but I have had to write this account entirely from memory and without the assistance of any notes for reference, so minor inaccuracies and omissions must be excused. The next phase of the fighting I saw from a more parochial outlook, but I have tried to fit in the general trend of operations, as a background to my own experiences, so I hope it may prove of some historical interest.

Apart from working in the War Room we were responsible for our own staff duties, but mine pretty well closed down. I was, however, responsible for the protection of the headquarters against attack by paratroops, and in this connection, I took over a paper scheme that had been compiled by a board of officers before the war started. None of the posts, nor the communications nor the troops to man them existed, except on paper, so I scrapped the whole scheme and started afresh. The troops available for the duty varied daily and they were an odd assortment, including first reinforcements and R.A.F.

One of my first acts was to turn the golf club house into a strong point. I told the secretary about this and he said it would require a special committee meeting! The next thing I did was to cut down a whole lot of banana trees, which gave excellent cover within bombing range of the outer-buildings. I was told this would require written permission from the competent authority! You just wouldn't have believed there was a war on. One afternoon, whilst going round the posts checking fire effect, I stopped at an ack-ack light machine-gun post, manned by such a 'hopeless looking aricle' in the R.A.F. that I asked him if he knew how to fire his gun. He didn't. I very much doubted whether he knew how to pull a cracker!

When I was off duty I used to whip down to our house which had developed into a kind of officers' hostel. Bill Waller, my G.S.O.3, took up residence with us and either he or I were always coming in or going out at odd hours of the night. Desmond Sheane, who was at rear-headquarters (the old Command Headquarters), was a kind of honorary member, as were Kenneth Selby Walker and his delightful wife, Emma. Kenneth was Number One of Reuters so kept no sort of hours at all and Emma used to park herself on us. Alison did wonders, nursing her baby and producing food at all hours of the day or night for unspecified numbers. We had an ack-ack gun in the garden and nobody minded it less than Baby Caroline, who seemed to regard the whole war as the most enormous joke. Nevertheless, one morning, when I had come off duty at 8 a.m., I drove down to the town, after breakfast, and had Alison booked on the first available passage, as it was quite obvious to me that Singapore was going for six.

I had thought a great deal about this and when I was not on duty in the War Room or attending to the ground defences of the head-quarters, I used to study all manner of maps and charts and think out how we could best regain the initiative. If things were allowed to go on, as at present, we were bound to be defeated in detail. I knew enough about the topography of Singapore to convince myself that it would never withstand an attack from Johore, so the prospects were that, if one didn't have the fortune to be killed, one was almost certainly booked for captivity. This undignified fate I viewed with disfavour and I reckoned it warranted a biggish wager.

My plan, in brief, was to land a battalion behind the Jap lines and to harry their communications on the only two routes that crossed the Perak River. I reckoned that the Japs would be across the Perak River before Christmas but that their forward troops would be entirely dependent on these two routes about the time that the operation could materialise. This I put as about the New Year. As things turned out my forecast was correct; actually, rather on the pessimistic side, which would have given me a bit of time in hand. I hoped that not only would we be able to cut off the Jap forward troops from essential battle supplies but also that we would force them to detach a large force to clear their line of communications.

As a result of this diversion, I hoped that we might be able to counter-attack their foremost troops and defeat them in detail and thus regain the initiative on the main battle front. I never imagined that we would be able to extricate the raiding battalion but, if this counter-stroke was successful, they would automatically be relieved. At the worst, we stood to lose a whole battalion, at the best we might regain the initiative. A lot depended on whether the navy could land a unit at all. I was not in a position to know the answer to this, except from my general knowledge on the subject as an amateur longshore-man.

The organisation which I appreciated I required for this job was to include a Naval Commander, an Army Commander and a topo-graphical Intelligence Officer. The Naval Officer would have to say how near the larger area he could put us ashore and also the times of landing and re-embarkation. The Army Commander would issue the detailed orders and tasks for the troops ashore, from the time they landed till the time they were to re-embark, based on my general di-rective for the conduct of operations ashore. The topographical Intel-ligence Officer would need to be a civilian. He would be responsible for producing all the local information regarding tides, waterways and possible landing places for the navy, and similar inland topographical details for the soldiery. He would also be responsible for the provision of guides and interpreters with the requisite local knowledge, and would have his own little staff.

I had completed the detailed proposal of my plan by December 17th and, that evening, I told Alison that I had thought out an opera-tion that gave some faint prospect of success if only someone would listen to it; and I told her more or less what it was all about. Alison, who always went pretty big, said, 'Now, what you ought to do is to tell the general about this'. I pointed out that this was not allowed as it was quite unconstitutional for a G.S.O.2 to approach a general direct.

'On the other hand,' I added, 'if I do this through the proper chan-nels the Japs will be at the Johore Straits before the general has even heard about it.'

'Well,' said Alison, 'in that case I would go and see the general di-rect. After all, you can only get flung out of Command H.Q., at the worst, and I know nothing would please you more than that.'

And so, we went on talking till I found myself ringing up the A.D.C. I told him I wanted an audience with the general and would he ask the G.O.C. if I could come round and see him. Ian Stonor, who was in my regiment, said he would go and find out. There was a long delay.

'Look, Angus, is this anything to do with the defence of H.Q.?'

'No, Ian, it bloody well isn't—it's a lot more important.'

'Well, just hold on, old boy—I'll go and find out.'

When I arrived at Flagstaff House I was ushered into the dining-room where the G.O.C. was seated with Captain Tennant, R.N., late of the *Repulse*.

'Sit down, Rose,' said the general. 'Now—what's all this about?'

I outlined my plan and the staff organisation that I thought necessary. The general meditated for a bit and then, smiling, turned to Captain Tennant.

'What do you think of the idea, Tennant?' he said.

'Seems a good idea to me,' replied the sailor.

'The idea's all right, Rose,' said the general, 'but you've got the staff organisation in existence already. The A.A.G. has all that laid on.' Then, turning to Tennant, 'Have you got any officer who you think could run the naval side?'

'Plenty of them. I can think of an excellent chap straight away.'

'All right,' said the general. 'You seem to have the right offensive spirit, Rose, so you can run the show yourself. Tell the B.G.S. tomorrow morning, that you're to be given every assistance over this and I will fix the final details when I get back from Kuala Lumpur in three days' time. Now, Ian, we must be off or we'll miss the train. Don't forget the Tommy gun.' And with that the general sped off in his car together with his A.D.C., leaving Captain Tennant and me together. I went into more details of my proposals with the sailor and he was encouraging from the naval point of view. We then climbed into my car and motored round to see the A.A.G. The A.A.G. thought I had gone clean nuts. He said he knew nothing about any organisation for amphibious operations, and he finished by saying that he couldn't help in any way at all.

On the way back, Tennant said he didn't think that I would ever be able to launch my scheme in the big way I intended and he advised me only to try for a modest force as, otherwise, it would probably end in the whole show being cancelled. I pointed out that a small raiding party could hardly produce decisive results and that what the hell did it matter if we did lose a whole battalion. We discussed the pros and cons far into the night and I was very grateful for the sympathy and understanding which the sailor displayed. His parting words, when I took my leave, were, 'Well, good luck, but take my advice and don't go too big or you won't have your party at all'.

It was about 2 a.m. when I got back and Alison was waiting up for me in her dressing gown. We had a drink together and talked it all over. Alison was worth all the rice in China on occasions such as these.

The next morning I clocked in bright and early at the War Room, and told the G.S.O.1 of my activities the previous night. He asked me since when I thought my middle name was Wavell and concluded by saying that he'd speak to the brigadier about it when he arrived.

It was not my tour of duty so, after flicking over all the situation reports and gleaning the latest information, I sat down in a chair and watched the minutes slowly ticking past. Eventually the brigadier arrived and, noticing him and the G.1 in confidential session, I tactfully glanced the other way. After some quite considerable time I was called over and told to explain myself. I did this as briefly as I could and then the B.G.S. sucked his pipe in silent meditation for what seemed hours. When the silence was broken, it transpired that he was not amused by my strategy. He would speak to the general on his return, not only about my strategy but also about my unbecoming conduct. In the meantime, I would continue to do duty in the Operations Room and that would be all.

One thing which I had learned in my twelve years' service was to accept a 'whortleberry' from my superiors in a gentlemanly fashion and, although I retired dispirited from the interview, the cordial relations that existed between the B.G.S. and myself were in no way impaired by this episode. I should have done exactly the same if I'd been in his shoes. Nevertheless, it was galling for me at the time and my immediate reaction was to withdraw to a corner and brood. Whilst thus engrossed, a young bearded Lieut.-Commander, with a twinkle in his eye, whom I recognised as a survivor from *Repulse* came up and said, 'Cheer up, chum, the war's not over yet'.

'No, but it soon will be,' I replied, 'and all I shall see of it is this Goddamned planning room.'

After that we got talking and I told him the whole story of my rejected plan.

'Victor Clarke's my name and you'll be seeing more of me later. Cheerio, chum, I'm off to see "Rammy".' With that he disappeared at full speed. 'Rammy' was the Rear-Admiral Malaya.

Victor was certainly right about seeing more of me later. He was back in the Operations Room, that night, during my tour of duty.

'I have seen "Rammy" and Tennant,' he said, 'and this party's going to be on; believe me. "Rammy" has given me the job and I'm starting in on it tomorrow.'

The next two days, when I was not on duty, I used to crack off to the naval base with Victor and discuss plans. In the evenings he used to come round to the house and he and I would go into a huddle whilst Alison carried on dispensing hospitality to all the casual visitors. On December 19th, the G.O.C. returned. I was called over and told officially that my plan was approved.

'Now what about troops;' said the G.O.C.

'Ah'm, sir,' I started—and Captain Tennant's last words came back to me, 'Well, I suppose a company would be better than nothing'.

'And where are we going to get a company from;'

'Singapore Fortress;' I queried.

'I don't think the Fortress Commander would take to that suggestion very readily. He wants more than he's got already.'

'In that case, sir, it only leaves the A.I.F., as 3rd Corps obviously can't spare a sausage; but I'd prefer British troops if I can get 'em.'

'It looks as if the A.I.F. are the only possible source,' said the general, after a few moments' consideration. 'I'll get on to General Gordon Bennett and find out if he will help us.'

Later on, I was told to go over to Johore Bahru and see the Australian commander. I discussed the project with him and he agreed to produce fifty men and three officers but no more. These he said could arrive at Kuala Lumpur by December 23rd. I, in my turn, undertook to fit them out with everything they wanted in the way of arms and equipment and promised to see that they would be well cared for. With the contingent offered me I could form two composite platoons; enough to put one platoon on each road. 'Rammy' was going to give me two platoons of Royal Marines but they wouldn't be ready till the New Year because, as yet, they were completely unacquainted with what a jungle even looked like.

I went home in high spirits and was the envy of Bill Waller and Desmond Sheane. The next two days I worked like a black laying on Tommy guns, grenades, prismatic compasses and all the other things we wanted. On the evening of December 21st, we had a farewell dinner party at home, after which I bid what I imagined would be a last farewell to Alison. She had been a brick about the whole show and just what a soldier's wife should be. Men get all the adventure and excitement; women the anxiety, the waiting and often the sorrow.

Desmond drove me to the station, which we reached in time to allow for a quick one in the Pullman bar before the train departed. Unfortunately, there was an air alert as soon as we reached the station and this seriously interfered with the drinking as the custodian of the bar went to ground with the keys. However, the departure of the train was correspondingly delayed, after the 'All Clear', so we were able to reach our modest target figure of two whiskies and sodas apiece.

There were two or three officers on the train whom I knew, including one Barney Tormey who used to introduce himself as such, adding 'Cornell, United States Artillery'. Barney was the United States Military Observer in Malaya Command. As G.S.O.2 Training, I used to take him about with me to watch exercises, and he was a most entertaining companion with a useful capacity for 'Scotch'. He used to spend a lot more time in the Forward Battle Area than his job of military observer demanded.

Victor Clarke boarded the train at the naval base and we joined up on the platform at Kuala Lumpur, early next morning, where we were met by a staff officer who conducted us to 3rd Corps Headquarters.

As soon as it became clear that my operations were to be limited to the activities of a minor force I decided to recast my plans. I had discussed the naval side in detail with Victor and he was able to assure me that, by using light motor craft, he would be able to put my troops ashore at places in the proximity of my target area. I therefore decided to carry out a series of hit and run raids in which we would aim at infiltrating small parties who would ambush the main roads over a period of thirty-six hours and then withdraw to rest and replenish, prior to another spring.

On arrival at 3rd Corps Headquarters I was interviewed by General Sir Louis Heath. I told the general of my intentions and added that Malaya Command had appointed me as G.S.O.2, Special Operations, to his headquarters, with instructions that I was to receive all my operational directives and tasks from him.

Old 'Piggy' Heath said, 'Well, Angus, I like your ideas; you have obviously given the matter some thought so you can have *carte blanche* to go right ahead. Let my staff know of anything you want and you shall have it'. To be given responsibility like this bucked me up no end, and I left the general's office feeling as happy as a sand-boy. The general's staff officers were as good as his word and, by that evening, I had collected an invaluable assortment of stuff including six Europeans from the local volunteers, who had lived in and around the target area; a large supply of Bata's hockey boots; anything in the way of rations which I asked for; map cases with cut and glued maps inside them of the target area; a medical detachment, and all my requirements in stores, weapons, ammunition and equipment. We had a Tommy gun for every other man and two oil compasses for each section. In fact, the only thing we lacked was a hunting parson, but I doubt if there were any in Malaya. In the meantime, Victor had gone through to establish himself at Port Swettenham. We had selected this place as the furthest advanced base from which we could operate. Unfortunately, the Japs had also selected it as a suitable daily bombing target at about the same time.

We had considered operating from Medan, in Sumatra, which was about equal distance to Swettenham from the target area (the distance being, in each case, about 120 odd miles), but we had ruled out the former on account of other difficulties and agreed that it was preferable to accept the inevitable bombing at the latter.

At Swettenham, Victor set about similar duties to those in which I was engaged at Kuala Lumpur. We had a coastal steamer, called the *Kudat,* as a base ship from which to operate. She arrived about December 23rd, and the motor launches followed her. Victor had more difficulty with his local guides than I did and, on Christmas Eve, he had to undertake a very lengthy motor drive with the declared intention of kidnapping the only *Serang* in the neighbourhood who was known to be reliable on the creeks which we intended to work. Needless to say, Victor was entirely successful.

On the morning of December 23rd, I met my Australians who arrived by the early train. We put the warriors into some huts near the station and I took their commander off to my room at the Station Hotel. After breakfast, I explained the scope of our operations to him and outlined the plan for the first raid, which I intended to launch on Christmas Day.

Gordon Bennett had already stipulated that I was subject to the normal procedure under which British officers were not empowered to give orders to or command Australian troops; so, apart from holding direct responsibility for putting them ashore and re-embarking them, my duties only extended to planning. However, I considered it essential that I should take part in the actual raid itself so that I should glean the necessary knowledge and experience for planning subsequent operations, in which the marines would be included. It was, therefore, agreed that I should attach myself to one of the two platoons in the capacity of an observer and that, as such, I should be entitled to perform the offensive duties of a private soldier.

After breakfast, we walked over to join the remainder of the troops who were at work cleaning weapons, preparing ammunition and filling magazines. The two other officers were introduced to me and I was tacked on to No. 1 platoon which was commanded by a young subaltern, freshly commissioned from an O.C.T.U., who was commonly known as 'Sandy'. The fifty men were volunteers from the six Australian battalions in Malaya and their glistening brown torsos were hard and well developed—good material.

About noon an endless length of ambulance train rumbled slowly into the station and stopped. The men ceased work and stared at the train, glancing almost shyly at each other meanwhile. I assessed the morale effect of this incident as not inconsiderable. Apart from serving as a grim reminder of the dangers that lay ahead, the train seemed to introduce an atmosphere of gloom and despondency. Victorious armies and conquering hosts no doubt acquire the morale stimulation of martial music, waving flags and cheering crowds, as a prelude to battle, but in defeat and withdrawal there is none of this.

As I was very anxious to obtain news of my regiment I went over to the platform and inquired from an orderly in the rear coach if there were any Argylls on board.

'Argylls,' said the orderly. 'Yes, sir, we're stuffed full of Argylls. Here's a Jock right 'ere.'

'Aye, surr,' added the Jock. 'There's nothing but Argylls aboard. They canna' keep the battalion fighting on ony mair like this. We've nae had a rest since it a' started and the cooks and all o' us is fightin' like the rest. Aye, and ye' canna' get the curnel to wear his tin hat. He just wears his Glengarry same as he was in barracks.'

I walked up the whole length of the train. Apart from Argylls, of whom there were a large number on board, there were also a good many Indian troops. The atmosphere was like a Turkish bath and the poor nursing sisters looked as if they were at the end of their tether. I met Bobbie Kennard of my regiment, lying up in the front coach and clad in a lance-corporal's shirt. He had commanded C Company on their independent role against the vastly superior Jap forces advancing down the Grik Road. C Company had fought with great distinction and had held the fort till the remainder of the battalion could be released to relieve the pressure.

Bobby had a bullet wound in the thigh, but seemed cheerful enough and had had a miraculous escape. He gave me an account of the fighting and then borrowed ten dollars off me. I never expected to see those ten bucks again but, nevertheless, I did; for Bobby returned his debt in Singapore some two months later! There was another Argyll, called Maclean, lying below Bobby. He was badly wounded and, though smilingly cheerful, looked terribly weak and frail. Poor Maclean succumbed to his wounds a day or two later. An ambulance train is not a pretty sight and I was never able to look at wounded men without being affected, although I soon grew accustomed to corpses, even when they were badly mutilated. After all, the dead cannot feel.

On the evening of December 24th I moved to Port Swettenham and set up my headquarters in the *Kudat,* where Victor had already hoisted his flag. The Australians came over on the same day and I had them billeted in a Seamen's Mission where they were quite comfortable. We had to put back 'Day One' from Christmas Day till Boxing Day as there was a delay in the arrival of our second motor launch from Singapore. This delay was just as well because we had a lot of preparations to complete before the troops were ready to embark.

During the course of my work at Kuala Lumpur I came in contact with a guerrilla organisation under the inspiring leadership of Colonel Warren of the Royal Marines. This organisation was directly under the control of G.H.Q., Far East, and, as far as I was able to ascertain, it contained two main elements. On the one side, there were the Chinese Communists and on the other a small and select band of highly skilled adventurers. The latter category included some remarkable personalities of whom I especially remember Freddie Chapman and a man called Gavin. Freddie took a long walk across the Perak River, at the time of our raid, as a result of which he wrote an exact and illuminating intelligence report.

Gavin always walked about with his pockets stuffed full of gelignite and other kinds of lethal instruments, but he was by no means a swashbuckler, on the contrary, rather a lone and elusive wolf. Warren himself had so many characteristics that it is hard to say which predominated. In the first place, he was incredibly ubiquitous; a master of time and space. He was fearless, but too intelligent to be foolhardy. In manner, he was upright, downright, and straightforward, and in appearance he was hard, handsome, and immaculate.

The Chinese Communists gave the appearance of making no sense at all but, in point of fact, they had a fine organisation. Their leader, who was the biggest swivel-cum-wall-eyed, genial-faced-cut-throat that it has ever been my lot to encounter, produced for my edification some impressive figures of the number of left-behind parties that would be working on the Jap line of communications at specified dates. I asked him if he didn't think that these figures were a bit optimistic. 'No, no,' he replied. 'All this we have already organised for many years to use against you British, but now we prefer to fight with you against the Japs'. With that he smilingly indicated two caricatures which adorned the walls of his office. One was Joe Stalin, the other Winston.

Small formations of Jap aircraft made low-level attacks each morning on Port Swettenham. This was my first experience of air attack (except for the initial raid on Singapore, which I didn't count, as nothing fell near me) and it was not nearly so frightening as I imagined it would be. The Japs were delivering low-flying cannon attacks for the most part and I, personally, prefer this type to the dive-bombing variety which is considerably more noisy. There was really too much work to do to think about the air raids but, on Christmas Day, Victor and I had time to accept an invitation to split a bottle of *Clicquot* with the manager of the Burma Oil Installation. Immediately after this I had the misfortune to enter a building that was serving the purpose of the local mortuary. Alas, my poor *Clicquot!* Although I got used to the sight of corpses I never got used to the smell. It's the same the whole world over, but it hits harder in tropical climates.

When the plan of operations for the raid was finally completed it was explained in detail to all ranks and it can best be summarised in three phases.

In phase one, the navy were to take us by motor launch from Port Swettenham to a predetermined place off the mouth of the Trong River, which was the closest point inshore that the draught of the motor launches would permit. This spot was known as Point W, to stand for 'where the hell are we?' At Point W we were to transfer from the launches into the motor boats and these boats were to take us up to a little village called Sungei Trong which boasted a small jetty. My fifty Australians were divided into two platoons each with three European interpreters-cum-guides. Each platoon was allotted one motor launch and each motor launch was assigned two motor boats. The motor boats had already been taken up under cover of darkness and left, with crews, in the Bernam River, which was approximately half-way. We were to leave Port Swettenham in the forenoon of Boxing Day, pick up the motor boats at dusk that night and take them in tow to Point W. At first light the following day we were to tranship, from the launches to the motor boats, and the boats were to put us ashore at Trong jetty between 0800 and 0900 hours: the latter being the time of high tide.

In phase two, one platoon was to move, across country, north-east-wards, to the area of Bukit Bubu Pass and the other platoon south-wards to the area of the hilly country in the vicinity of Bukit Rengam. Each platoon commander had complete liberty of action in his target area but there was to be no shooting within a prescribed zone near the landing point, except in the case of enemy interference, in which case we were to fight our way through to the boats. The platoons were to rendezvous at Trong jetty at 2200 hours the following day, which was half an hour before high tide. The navy were to give us an hour's grace at Trong, and if we failed to turn up that night, we had a second appointment with them before high water the following night.

Phase three was merely an inverted form of phase one. During phase two the motor boats were to tie up in the mangrove swamps, whilst the motor launches were to disperse seawards. These plans sound simple enough but the detailed scheming of the operations involved a great deal of hard work and juggling to get the correct answers from the factors of time and space.

On Christmas night, we had a modest supper in the *Kudat's* saloon. Peace on earth and goodwill towards all men. 'What a very remote doctrine,' I thought. Anyhow, it clashed violently with my professional aspirations for the forthcoming raid. I went to bed as soon as I had swallowed my sardine on toast and slept like a log.

BRITISH TROOPS ON THE MARCH

CHAPTER 5

The Temerloh Raid

Some months after the fall of Singapore I came across the following account of operations in Malaya in the *Weekly Times* (about February 3rd, 1942):

AN ACCOUNT OF A COMMANDO RAID IN MALAYA

A Commando in Malaya—Behind the Enemy Lines—Australian Bushcraft

Singapore, January 8th, 1942

A war correspondent of the *Straits Times,* in a dispatch published today, described how Australian troops now in action in North Malaya are ranging behind the Japanese lines as a small commando unit, whose object is to sabotage the enemy's communications, to destroy his material, and kill his men.

By ways and means undisclosed these troops find their way behind the enemy lines. Once there they are entirely dependent on themselves.

'Sometimes', continues the correspondent, 'they have to shoot their way out, but for the most part they seek to keep under cover, cause the utmost damage of which they are capable, and then return to the comparative safety of our front lines. All the men in this unit are handpicked. For the most part they are a fine, sturdy type of Australian bushmen, although one with whom I spoke was an 18-year-old city lad from Sydney. Well versed in bushcraft and skilled in taking the fullest advantage of the country for cover and for sustenance, they constitute ideal troops for this hazardous work in which they are greatly assisted by three Malayan planters who act as interpreters and guides.'

The correspondent describes one incident for which the unit was responsible. Effectively hidden in dense jungle on either side of an important road they saw a Japanese staff car driving along at an even speed. How safe the enemy felt was shown, by the fact that the car was flying the Japanese Army pennant. A Japanese major-general was among the staff officers in the car. 'As the enemy drove through the Australians' position', says the correspondent, 'all hell was let loose. The incident was over in a couple of seconds. The car swerved, skidded, and hurtled into a ditch where it capsized. Subsequent examination of the wreckage showed that all the occupants of the vehicle had been killed outright either by bullets or exploding grenades.'

'On this particular sortie', says the correspondent, 'the unit was well behind the Japanese lines for several days. For the most part the men travel as light as possible, the bulk of their equipment consisting of arms and ammunition, supplemented by a water bottle. For food, they depend solely on the country in which they are travelling.'

I recognised this as bearing a strong similarity to the Temerloh party but I don't think anyone of that raiding force could claim that this was the truth, the whole truth and nothing but the truth, so the full story should now be told.

The troops were timed to arrive on the quayside at 10:00 hours on Boxing Day and, at that moment, twenty-four Japanese fighter bombers droned into sight from north-westwards. The troops were tactically dispersed and all ack-ack light machine-guns mounted. In addition to this there was a good deal of 'flak' in the dock area, including a lot of ack-ack L.M.G.s on the naval craft and also sixteen Bofors guns and two sections of 3.7-inch. The Jap planes circled round at a high ceiling and then swooped down like so many hawks on their prey. *Brrrrrmph-Brrrrrmph-Brrrrrmph* went the sticks of bombs, followed by columns of debris and smoke. In no time aircraft were flying round in all directions at varying altitudes.

There was a continuous yattering of light and heavy machine guns. Bullets were whipping, cracking and thudding all over the place. I was sitting on the edge of a shallow drain with my back to a *godown* and facing towards the river. The *Kudat* was within a stone's-throw to my left front. One Jap plane, low enough to knock your hat off, came

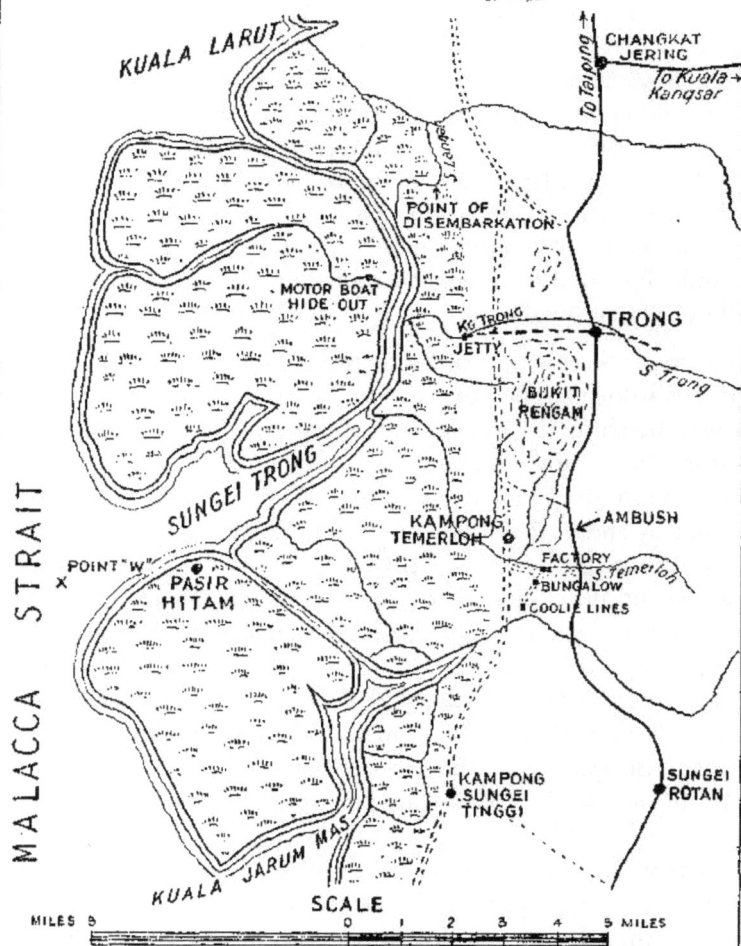

TRONG AREA (4°40'N., 100°40'E.), PERAK, MALAYA.
FROM A SKETCH BY THE AUTHOR, DRAWN FROM MEMORY.

MAIN ROADS
TRACKS OR ESTATE ROADS
JUNGLE TRAILS
MANGROVE SWAMP

KUALA LARUT

CHANGKAT JERING

To Taiping →

To Kuala Kangsar →

POINT OF DISEMBARKATION

S. Lenang

MOTOR BOAT HIDE-OUT

Kg. TRONG

TRONG

JETTY

S. Trong

BUKIT RENGAM

SUNGEI TRONG

KAMPONG TEMERLOH

← AMBUSH

FACTORY

S. Temerloh

POINT "W"
X

PASIR HITAM

BUNGALOW

COOLIE LINES

MALACCA STRAIT

KAMPONG SUNGEI TINGGI

SUNGEI ROTAN

KUALA JARUM MAS

SCALE

MILES 5   0   1   2   3   4   5 MILES

across the estuary straight for a Bofors gun which was mounted a bare hundred yards to my right. I had already mentally put this bird in the bag. *Pomph-Pomph-Pomph-Pomph-Pomph*, spoke the Bofors—not a scratch. *Pheew-Brrumph*—and a bomb registered a fairly near miss on *Kudat*. The sky was speckled with the white and black puffs of the Bofors and 3.7-inch explosions. One or two fires had started in the dock area. A Jap plane was winging it out to sea with a long plume of white smoke from its tail—for all the world like a duck, with a leg down.

I was absorbed in the spectacle when I heard a roar like the end of creation, at my back, and I turned, expecting to see the *godown* and myself disappear into eternity. Instead, a Jap plane skimmed the roof and banked steeply to port on meeting the full force of *Kudat's* L.M.G.s. I might have had a slap at this intruder with my Tommy gun but I was a bit slow on the draw and he was round the back of another *godown* before I was on to my mark. The raid seemed to last only a very short time. An odd plane still hung about but we closed the troops, checked over ammunition expenditure and embarked straight away.

I had attached myself to the platoon which was allotted the area of Bukit Bubu Pass as I knew the country from having motored through it on several occasions, whilst driving from Penang to Ipoh. Funnily enough the first time I passed a certain spot on this road I had some kind of indescribable feeling of familiarity with it. I knew I could never have seen it before and, although I was not a believer in re-incarnation, I vaguely sensed that I was connected with it through another life. This feeling was so strong that I mentioned it to my companion. When I had been discussing the details of the topography with the planters I suggested this place as being an ideal site for an ambush and all were agreed it was probably the most favourable one in the area. I had an overwhelming sensation that Fate demanded of me that I should go to this place for some purpose or other but, at the same time, I had no premonition of death. It so turned out that I made two attempts in all to get to this spot but failed to make the grade on both occasions, due to circumstances beyond my control. This was so nearly 'an extraordinary coincidence' that I must apologise to any reader who may be disappointed that the circumstance was not brought to some logical conclusion.

Once on board, we were soon under way and I got the platoon commander, the section commanders and guides down into the cabin to study the map and try and learn it off by heart. Whilst so engaged, a wayward Jap aircraft dived down and cannoned us but we threw him off without difficulty and suffered no damage. The rest of the day we lolled about on deck watching the clear, deep-blue, foam-flecked water gliding past. The sea, below the surface, was a mass of jelly-fish and I viewed the prospect of a swim with intense displeasure. Intermittently throughout the day, the galley, which was about the size of a lavatory cupboard, produced welcome tea and to this we added our rations of bully beef and biscuits. I have never had an appetite before point-to-points, athletic meetings, Rugger matches and such like. Apparently, battles were to be no exception to this rule.

By dusk we were hove-to off the mouth of the Bernam River and number one and number two motor boats were soon sighted heading in our direction. We made fast the tow to our launch, but there was no sign of the other two boats. We hailed a small motor boat which was cruising not far off and the skipper informed us that he had seen a couple of motor boats up the Bernam River which were high and dry at low tide. Old Victor went clean off the deep end. His parting instructions to the petty officers of the motor boats were that they must not beach till low tide. Now the stupid clots had piled themselves on the putty, when the tide was ebbing, and it would be full flow before they were off. Our timetable allowed for no such acts of neglect and stupidity as this.

The owner of the small motor boat said he could help us out by producing a craft that would take twenty-five men and perhaps some more with a squash. This was better than nothing but of course the new craft was neither provisioned nor crewed and it also took more draught than we wanted. Anyhow, the new boat was eventually found, and brought alongside. The engine seemed highly unreliable.

Whilst thus engaged in procuring substitute craft a heavy thundering sound of high-powered engines became apparent to the south. Shortly afterwards a Fairmile (R.A.F. crash-boat) was identified and, as she drew up alongside, I recognised the martial bearing of the figure amidships as that of Colonel Warren.

Only Warren could have arrived like this.

He was, apparently, on his way to one of the Sembilan Islands to investigate and eliminate a Jap transmitting station that was alleged to be working there.

I had a long chat with Warren, on board his Fairmile, whilst we were waiting for the newly-acquired motor boat to materialise. He was not very optimistic on our account and considered it most audacious for an officer of my experience to meddle with amphibious operations. He cheered me up a bit by summarising the type of things the Japs would do to us if they succeeded in taking us prisoner, and concluded by saying that if we managed to pull it off Victor and I would certainly get something out of it.

The motor-boat *Myrtle* was now taken in tow and we continued our trip onwards to Point W, under the cover of darkness. I shaved overnight and then packed up my few valuables such as a cigarette case, my note-book and some private papers, all of which I left in the cabin. When I woke up the next morning it felt like the last day of the holidays, before going back to school—perhaps not quite so bad as that.

I was on the bridge a good hour before first light and Victor was displaying some concern as to the navigation. The first streaks of dawn silhouetted the high features of Bukit Bubu against the eastern sky. Some calculations were made and Victor announced that he reckoned we were plumb on the top of Point W. I agreed and expressed my appreciation for a masterly bit of driving on his part.

The motor boats were brought alongside and we packed in like sardines. We then cast adrift and waited for *Myrtle* to start up and join us. Nothing happened. Victor hailed me from the flagship.

'*Myrtle* won't start up. What are we going to do?'

'We'll just have to do the raid with one platoon,' I called back. 'Won't she really start? Oh, Hell! Oh ...'

'Start up,' I ordered.

'Good Luck, chum,' called Victor. 'See you midnight tomorrow.'

I am very superstitious that when things go wrong they happen in threes. Now two things had gone wrong. First, number three and four boats had stuck on the putty. Secondly, *Myrtle* had let us down with a thump. What was the third to be?

We chugged on up the river towards Trong jetty. It was about ten miles upstream and we were making five knots on a flowing tide. This was good enough and would leave us nearly an hour in hand. The sun was now topping the hills. A soft ground mist was rising up to gather in fleecy clouds midway between the level of the mangrove trees and the distant hills. The beauty of that morning made the killing that lay ahead seem rather remote. I wondered, vaguely, if I should ever see another dawn, and I was pleasantly surprised to find that the problem caused me no anxiety. I had none of that needle feeling which I had so often experienced before going into bat at cricket, or on the first tee at an important golf match. We clung to the friendly shadows cast by the mangrove trees on the eastern edges of the creek. The motor boats were well laden down and there was almost no free board on either craft.

We arrived, without incident, at the entrance of the creek which led to Trong jetty. As there was now only one platoon I decided that, instead of making for the jetty, we would go up the Sungei Langat, as this would take us two miles nearer our target area. We had with us a Malay *serang* who was an expert on the local creeks. He said he knew of a good landing place up the Langat and the sub-lieutenant said we were well in hand for time.

Shortly before reaching the Langat Creek, we met some natives in a couple of *sampans*. We stopped and inquired if they had any information about the Japanese. A more dismal collection of humans I have never met. They told us that they had come from Port Weld, which was under ten miles away and there, they said, the Japs were marshalling a fleet. They complained that all their rice had been confiscated and they were in a bad way. I handed out a suitable bribe, which didn't seem to cheer them up to any great extent, and this was the signal for our third disaster. Number two motor boat refused to start up. This meant a tow and the tow reduced our speed from about five knots to one knot. After about half a mile number two boat got going again and I heaved a sigh of relief, as we were now up against time and tide. I reckoned we would just make the distance but my hopes were unfounded for, after another half mile, the boat again conked out, ran aground and fouled her propeller.

I now had to make a snap decision on two alternatives. First, I could take on number one boat to the landing point, disembark and send the boat back to ferry the troops from number two boat forward. The danger of this plan was that the tide might ebb sufficiently far to prevent the ferry service from working. The other alternative was to leap out where we were and plough through the half mile of mangrove which lay between us and dry ground. As I was debating this project I noticed leaves were beginning to flow downstream. The tide was already ebbing. I decided on course two and ordered the troops to climb out. I am still in two minds as to whether or not I acted correctly and I think that only by actually carrying out each of the two courses open would it be possible to prove which was right and which was wrong.

Anyhow, one thing is certain and that is that the mechanical break-down of number two boat prejudiced the whole raid. To cross that odd half mile of mangrove on the map looked easy money. In practice, it was a very different kettle of fish. In the best going we were knee deep in mud. Every few score yards a creek would be encountered and here the mud was waist deep. The creeks, although only a few feet wide, had to be circumvented. Apart from mud we were lacerated by thorns and prickly shrubs and entwined by creepers. It took three hours to get through that half mile of mangrove and when we emerged on the coconut slopes I, for one, was quite ready for a rest.

Once the troops had disembarked my responsibilities were technically at an end. I was in authority for liaison between the army and the navy but ashore I was merely attached to the platoon for the purpose of gaining first-hand experience for planning subsequent raids. This was all very well in theory but in practice things were rather different and, when unforeseen circumstances arose, matters were often referred to me. In this case I would give my advice and then Sandy would make his decision.

As soon as we cleared the mangrove swamps a halt was called and a council of war held. The leading planter-guide, by name of Harvey, said that in his opinion we could no longer hope to make the distance to the Bukit Bubu Pass by dark that night. Van Rennan, the other planter, agreed. It was, therefore, decided that we would switch over to the other platoon's target area which was appreciably closer; something like ten miles instead of twenty. The revised plan, therefore, was to aim for the road in the vicinity of the south-eastern slopes of Bukit Rengam for an ambush that evening.

Shortly before one o'clock we went forward by compass march to hit off the bridle path which would lead us through Sungei Trong and thence southwards towards Temerloh. After meeting the bridle track we ran into numberless locals and, from them, we gathered that the Japs had a detachment at Trong and that they regularly ran a motor patrol between Trong and the jetty. It seemed possible that they might be using Trong jetty as riverhead of a supply line based on Port Weld. We took normal precautions crossing the Trong-Trong jetty road but saw no enemy and continued our advance without incident. After an hour's march, we halted in a little Malay village of some half-dozen houses. Here the locals gave us coconuts and sugar and our planters passed the time of day by talking to them in the vernacular. The natives were delighted to see us and wanted to know how soon we were going to return, to help them with their normal industries. They advised us that we must not go near the main road as it was packed with Japs and very dangerous and they said that off the road we were quite safe. I think we gave them ten dollars for our refreshment, but they gave us five back and insisted that this was more than liberal payment. During the whole time, we were behind the Jap lines I was most impressed by the way all the locals, whether Malays, Tamils or Chinese, declined to exploit us financially and, moreover, gave us every possible assistance within their power.

After our halt, it was agreed that we should not go through Temerloh village as, in the first place, this might lead to information regarding our presence reaching the Japs and, secondly, because there was a shorter route, marked on the map, leading from the bridle path eastwards to the main road, which skirted the southern shoulder of the Rengam feature. Although there was only one track marked on the map there were dozens on the ground and I was called on to decide if the one at which our point scouts had stopped was in fact the correct one. After some consideration, I decided it probably was, but the map was clearly out of date. In point of fact it was a 1915 survey, and the water courses and tracks had changed appreciably in the meantime. I was sufficiently experienced in jungle marching to appreciate the danger of following a track from a map but we were in very close jungle and, as movement off the track would have necessitated cutting, I decided to take a chance and follow the trail. After four or six hundred yards, I began to have my doubts.

After a mile, I realised that the path we were following was not shown on the map. I went on another half-mile in the hopes that we would be taken back into our course. By now we were in open jungle and compass march was a practical proposition. I headed on by compass and then we ran into a few native huts. The headmen informed us that there was no way of reaching the road at the south-eastern end of the Rengam Hill, except by going back the way we had come and thence onwards to Temerloh village, where we would have to turn east. The headman also told us we were mad to go anywhere near the main road as it was full of Japs.

I didn't believe this yarn about impenetrable forest between us and the road and I knew, again from experience, that natives are far from being experts on the jungle in their own localities. They know the tracks which they use for business and off these tracks they never venture. It could only be half a mile to the road through the jungle whereas, if we went by Temerloh, it was a good three to four miles and we had no idea of what might be in the village; possibly Japs, possibly spies. You just couldn't say.

Sandy was dead against taking a chance on compass marching, after our experiences in the mangrove swamps that morning, and after some deliberation he decided to turn back and make for Temerloh. We retraced our steps somewhat heavily and this had a depressing psychological effect on everyone. Our packs felt heavier and our feet more weary, and I sensed that I was held to be responsible for these effects.

On regaining the bridle track we called a short halt. I lay on my back with my legs propped up vertically against a tree, and this is a tip which I recommend to any weary-footed traveller. We continued after a few minutes and marched through Temerloh, where all the children burst into tears at the sight of us and fled screaming to hide in their mothers' *sarongs*.

In Temerloh, Sandy picked up a guide who said he would take us to the road. After a short distance, he indicated some telephone lines, on the far side of a rubber clearing, which he said marked the main road. This did not agree with my map, and it turned out to be an estate road running from the factory to the *coolie* lines.

By now it was after four o'clock. The troops were tired and would require rest before a fight, so Sandy decided to harbour in the coolie lines for the night. I suggested that he and his section commanders should reconnoitre an ambush for the morrow, before dark, so, whilst the platoon made for the *coolie* lines, we four went to the factory. Here we took a rest and had a Tamil *coolie* knock us down a couple of coconuts apiece.

Sandy started off on a very involved chiropody task and, wearying of this, I said I would go on by myself to see the form on the main road, leaving them to carry out their reconnaissance in their own time. I made off on a compass bearing to the south-east corner of Bukit Rengam. It was easy going through rubber-jungle and, after about thirty minutes, I almost stepped on to the road before noticing it. Here I selected a point of vantage, in the shade of the westering sun.

I was glad to be alone and to have the companionship of nature, and I thought what fun it would be to go on a party like this with a couple of friends; all of us sharing the same spirit of adventure. I was a stranger in this particular party. We lacked the advantages of having lived, trained, and played together; in consequence, we were not a

RSM SANDY MUNNOCH

team, and lacked that one essential quality of mutual confidence. The Australians, themselves, had the common bond of race, but they came from different units and lacked the precision and *esprit de corps* of a homogeneous body. We could not claim to be the same quality of men as Roger's Rangers, in *North-West Passage,* or as Wingate's men were to prove themselves to be in Burma. Of course, it takes time to build up units of this type, and we were a scratch force collected on the spur of the moment and not specially trained.

The place where I was sitting offered every facility for a successful ambush and subsequent getaway. I was figuring out a plan of how I would dispose my troops when I heard the sound of approaching transport. I crouched down in the shade with my heart pounding high up in my chest. Six or seven lorries disappeared in the direction of the front line. The sight of these vehicles was a tonic to my weariness and I was keyed up with excitement like a *débutante* at a ball. After a while, a signal maintenance party appeared on the scene. They had a truck and consisted of about half a dozen troops under an N.C.O. They were testing the telephone line and some of them were finely set up men; much taller than I imagined they would be.

After this nothing passed for some time and then a large party of about sixty cyclist troops came by. They wore a varied assortment of uniforms and headgear. Some of them had the dome-shaped helmet, some the *kepi* and some wide-brimmed *topees* of the missionary type. Some wore trousers, some shorts and singlets and some breeches and *puttees*. I noticed, with pleasure, that they all carried their rifles slung on their bicycles and I appreciated that there would be a considerable time lag before they would be able to return our fire in an ambuscade.

They were a motley collection of soldiery. They bicycled anyhow and not in half-sections. Many of them hummed to themselves as they pedalled along and they seemed in good spirits. One man's chain came off and he dismounted almost within spitting distance of me. The rest had passed on before he was ready. Had I been a real backwoodsman, I would have lassoed this Samurai and brought him back a captive or, alternatively, with a blow-pipe and a poisoned dart, I could have dealt him a shrewd blow in the seat of his pants, owing to the position which circumstances had forced him to adopt.

As time was now getting on I returned to our bivouac highly satisfied with the prospects for tomorrow. I called in at the factory to pick up my haversack which I had hidden in one of the troughs and, to my surprise, I found that Sandy's party had left their weapons and equip-

JAPANESE TROOPS ON BICYCLES

ment out in the open. Their negligence might result in our presence being disclosed and as I could not carry all the stuff myself I hid it carefully in the factory and struck a course for the *coolie* lines.

It was dark now and sentries had been posted. The troops had established cordial relations with the Tamils and quantities of tinned fruit, tea, sugar and pungent native cigarettes were forthcoming. The Tamils told us that the Japs had arrived on the estate the previous day and impounded all their rice without paying a cent of compensation. In our withdrawal through Malaya we had distributed all reserves of rice to the locals, instead of destroying them, through humanitarian motives, but the Japs merely exploited our policy by calling it all in as soon as they arrived.

Shortly after my arrival Sandy appeared with his party, expressing some concern at the disappearance of his Thompson gun. I was able to put the commander at his ease on this subject and this brought such relief to all concerned that no accusations were brought against my ancestry, which flattered me to the extent of borrowing a Tamil *coolie's* bicycle and setting off to retrieve the hidden goods. Two of the Diggers insisted on accompanying me on this mission and together we steered a wobbly course to the factory.

On returning to the *coolie* lines I found another council of war had taken place. Sandy had decided that it would be courting disaster to attempt an embarkation at Trong jetty the following night after making a kill in the vicinity of Temerloh that same morning. The revised plan, therefore, would be to lay an ambush shortly after dawn and then to make straight for Trong. Bill Harvey, one of the planters, was to go to Trong first thing in the morning, disguised as a Malay, and collect sufficient *sampans* for the party. He was also to find out where the motor boats were lying and we were to paddle downstream to this point.

I had hoped that we should be able to do three or at least two ambushes and I relied on a moderately safe chance of a getaway, owing to the time that it would take the Japs to organise patrol sweeps, some way back on their line of communications. If the worst came to the worst, we stood a fairly good chance of being able to shoot our way out. We had the initiative and it was never intended that this party should be a cake walk. My councils, however, were not entertained.

After supper, a fire was lit in front of which we hung our wet clothes and lay down to sleep. We spent a pretty uncomfortable night in filthy surroundings and were devoured by mosquitoes which seemed to find our protection cream much to their liking. I slept fairly well in short bursts of about twenty minutes and then awoke for an interlude of scratching. We got up at about 3 a.m. and I took a wash out of the local well which freshened me up. At 4 a.m. we moved off into the rubber, in anticipation of the Japs getting wind of our presence, in which case they would, no doubt, send out a fighting patrol to engage us at dawn. Once in the rubber, we sat down in a circle, facing outwards, till it became sufficiently light to move.

At the first signs of daylight we moved off through the rubber, on a compass bearing. The troops kept well spread out in their sections and moved quickly and silently. We crossed over the estate road by the rubber factory and went down over the Temerloh River. From thence we went north-eastwards through jungle country and across a number of wide streams till we came to the main road. The place where I had gone the previous evening was a little further north. It was now about 7.30 a.m.

We halted and sat down in the jungle, whilst the section leaders went forward with the platoon commander. One of the Australians turned to me and observed that it was a fine morning for a killing. I agreed, but omitted to add that it took more than a fine morning for this kind of job. The section commanders came back. My corporal asked me if I cared to take a hand and I was posted as left-hand man but two of the left-hand section, and indicated a tree for cover. I asked what orders there were and the section commander said, 'You don't have to bother about orders, Major'.

I said, 'Who is to open fire; What is the order to cease fire? Where is the rendezvous after the ambush? Have I any special task, except to open fire on the enemy?'

'You just shoot 'em up when the others do,' replied the corporal and with that he passed on to post the next man.

I now realised that the ambush consisted of a dead straight length of road lined, by the three sections of the platoon. There were no orders at all and a complete absence of any tactical plan. The field craft was not so hot either. The sun was low down and slap in our eyes and I thought that a little experience at decoying pigeon or flighting duck might teach the platoon commander some useful lessons in this kind of work.

I removed my tin hat as it was likely to give me away. In Malaya, we had not been provided with camouflage nets so our helmets could not be garnished with foliage. I also put down my haversack which was mighty heavy on my shoulder. This was a stupid thing to do, all the same, as will be seen later. It is worth mentioning here that we all had certain loads to carry and these we were allowed to wear in the way we thought best. The majority of us carried a bandolier, a slung haversack and a map case, if we had a map. The contents of my haversack consisted of five slides of Tommy gun ammunition, a full water bottle, a packet of dried raisins, a packet of biscuits, a first field-dressing, a tin or mosquito cream, a bottle or water purification tablets and a couple of grenades. The latter I transferred to my trouser pockets and I carried a rifle and bandolier of one hundred rounds of small arms ammunition, in addition. This was, actually, a great deal too much kit and, in the next raid, I cut it down drastically.

It is also my considered opinion that it always pays, in the end, to stick to the regulation skeleton equipment of belt and braces and carry what has to be carried on this framework. It is most important that the weight of the load is evenly distributed and not all taken on one bearing point. In my case, the bearing point was my shoulder and, after plugging along all the previous day with this load, I could feel the result.

We had been in position a fair time—about twenty minutes I should say—when the sound of vehicles could be heard approaching from our left. A fleet of touring cars then cruised past. They seemed to contain, for the most part, what looked like white-suited Malays. I caught a glimpse of an odd green Jap uniform, but the cars flashed past pretty quickly and I didn't get a very good view. I reckon that this party might possibly be an assortment of Quislings, working on behalf of the Commissariat Department. There was no shooting and I was glad of this as I didn't consider it a worthwhile target.

We had another longish pause, eventually broken by the rumble of transport coming from the direction of the Japs' front line. I waited with bated breath and judged the moment when the vehicles would be within the ambush layout. There was no shooting and I breathed a sigh of relief over this, as all that came past were two most enormous ambulances. They were as large as the biggest pantechnicon that you will ever see on the Great West Road. As this was to be the one and only drive of the day it would have been just too bad if the ambulances had been beaten up; rather analogous to coming back on the *twelfth* with nothing but a brace of hen pheasants.

I hoped we might get a nice cycling party next, like the one I had seen the night before. A bird came and perched on a bough near my stand. He preened himself a bit and then started tuning in. There wasn't a sound of a living being within miles. This was thrilling work and incomparable to any other kind of sport, such as sitting up for tiger. Furthermore, it was all being paid for by King George. I thought of a bleak winter morning on the Solway, ten years ago, when I was lying out on the mud flats with a brother officer hoping to kill my first goose. The sound of approaching vehicles gave the same thrill as I had experienced when I heard the honking gaggles heading in my direction. I would have liked that same brother officer to have been with me now. I would have liked to have organised this whole ambush with him. I fancy it would have made some sense. This ambush was making no sense at all.

I decided to go down and have a word with Sandy as I suddenly had a hunch that the whole thing was going to be a complete flop.

I had gone about thirty yards or so when I heard more vehicles approaching from our end of the ambush, so I flattened myself against a tree. As the leading car flashed into sight I saw a blue pennant flying on the radiator cap. I thought instinctively—'Brigadier!—We must have him,' and, in the split second which I had for making a decision, I put up my rifle, swung through on to the driver and pressed the trigger. 'Correct!' The driver crumpled up, the car flashed out of sight, the tyres screamed on the tarmac and the vehicle crashed into the ditch further down the road. I was quite pleased with my marksmanship and got a kick out of my shot akin to pulling down a high pheasant at a covert shoot. The fact that I was standing up made it considerably easier and I have an idea that in a cramped sitting position I would probably have registered a washout. Behind this first car a whole fleet of vehicles pulled up. They must have been driving at very close density.

No sooner had the first car crashed to a standstill than, to quote the *Times* correspondent, 'all hell was let loose'. Tommy guns, rifles and grenades crashed out in perfect harmony. I fired two more aimed shots at individuals and then got a jam through a piece of creeper engaging with my bolt action. I had not been taught how to cure this variety of jam in my young days at Hythe and my fingers turned into thumbs. I eventually got my breach clear and fired two more 'browning' shots at driver's cabs but, by this time, there was so much smoke about that it was impossible to see. There was a good deal of shouting going on now, and someone called out, 'Look out for the flanks.'

Some of the troops were still shooting and others now started to withdraw. One thing that stood out quite clearly was that control had broken down and no one had any idea of their duties. I was at a loss as to the next move myself so I went down the line and hailed Sandy. As I came up to him he said, 'Jesus, we didn't half crack the bastards'. I agreed and said, 'Now, what about slipping back via the *coolie* lines and giving the bastards another crack further down the road'.

We were standing, now, in the jungle, about twenty to thirty yards from the road. Bob Van Rennan was with us. The other troops were disappearing in the direction from which we had come, or else had already disappeared. A motor horn was letting forth a series of long blasts. Someone on the road was roaring like the Bull of Bashan. Sandy said, 'To Hell, we're getting out of this as quick as God will let us'. I caught a glimpse of what I thought was a figure, slipping between the trees on the road and took aim in the kneeling position, but I saw nothing more. Sandy said, 'Come on, let's get on, there's no point in hanging around'. I said I had left my helmet and haversack near the road and wanted to get them.

Sandy said if I got fixed up getting my tin hat it was none of his business, and I rather agreed with him. I told him to go on and rally the platoon. I couldn't find my hat and haversack and I got into a black rage with myself as it is pretty degrading to turn up short of equipment. I caught up with the others, about half a mile from the road. They were just crossing a stream. Sandy said there were no absentees. I felt like a nudist at a garden party with neither my helmet nor haversack. I still had my map case and compass and there was nothing of value in my haversack, but it was a poor show all the same.

We continued heading due west and after a very short time hit the bridle path between Sungei Trong and Temerloh. Here we turned right handed and, after a bare hundred yards, came to the spot where I had taken the wrong turning the previous afternoon. I had not been so far wrong, after all. Furthermore, my decision to make for the road, by compass march, was proved correct. There was nothing but half a mile of rubber-jungle between where we had checked and retraced our steps, the previous day, and the main road.

Having struck the bridle track we headed due north and reached Sungei Trong about eleven o'clock. We stopped short of the village and dispersed in the coconuts. I had no confidence that the *sampan* idea would work, so I got hold of Sandy and suggested that we should rest where we were till the evening and then carry out another ambush at a place not very far distant. Sandy did not support this idea so I proposed we should call for volunteers, as I fancied we could do a very nice shoot-up with a handful of men. We were discussing this

103

project when Bill Harvey returned disguised, more or less, as a Malay. He said he had got everything arranged. The *sampans* were lined up ready to start and the motor boats had been located. Sandy said that, in this case, we would beat it.

We moved northwards, through the village, over the road the Japs were reputed to patrol, and struck the Trong River. The majority of the platoon crammed themselves into the available *sampans* and about half a dozen of us were left ashore, as there were insufficient paddles. Bill Harvey and Bob Van Rennan went off to collect more paddles and it now started to pour with rain. The water came down in solid sheets and ran off the plantain leaves as if so many taps had been turned on. This was most refreshing and I enjoyed a water bottle full of sweet fresh rain water. It was nectar and the best drink I had taken since the *Clicquot* on Christmas Day.

We waited for a long time and I was just wondering if something had not gone wrong when an Aussie came up and said that a Malay had told Harvey that there were some friends of ours in the village who wanted to see us. He said that Harvey and Van Rennan had gone to investigate and that he had come back to report. This seemed a bit of a mystery to me and, suspecting a possible trap, I wondered how we could best help. I didn't know where the two planters had gone and it was a bit of a problem.

Whilst cross questioning the Aussie I was relieved to see Harvey appear through the undergrowth, together with an amicable group of locals. The next thing I knew was that a heavily bearded Malay had slapped me on the back exclaiming at the same time, 'Oh, Christ! fancy meeting you here, Mr. Rose'. For a moment, I failed to recognise the identity of P.S.M. Love, of my own regiment, behind his natural disguise. Then, turning to a red-bearded Malay I extended a hand with the traditional observation of, 'Dr. Livingstone, I presume'.

'No, Surr, Seargent Skinner,' came the reply. 'Do you no mind when you wis ma' company commander in the machine gunners when we wis on the frontier?'

'Aye,' added Love. 'An' Mister Rose was ma platoon commander in twulve platoon when we was in Edinbrae'.

Our respective records of service seemed to be of considerably more importance than any current affairs. Skinner and Love can only be described as 'in cracking fine form'. They were exquisitely attired in high class Malayan clothes and Love had a pair of patent leather dancing pumps on his feet. These two had been cut off during the fighting on the Grik road about a fortnight earlier. They had come across country, towards the coast, and their adventures would fill a volume. With them they had a sergeant in the Leicestershire Regiment who had been cut-off at the Jitra battle on December 13th. Jitra was about 120 miles north of our present position.

Skinner said he was fed up with curry, in more senses than one, and Love introduced the Leicestershire man to me with all the formality of a sergeants' dance. It was a marvellous tonic to join up with men like these whom one knew and understood. The comradeship that exists between officers and N.C.O.s in the British Army is deep and sincere. I doubt if the same relationship of mutual respect and friendship can exist in any army but ours.

Paddles were now produced and we got aboard the four remaining *sampans*. I was in the last craft, together with Skinner and another man. The boat bore a certain resemblance to a sieve but, with one man paddling and the other two baling, we just managed to keep afloat. After a couple of hundred yards we started gaining on Love and the Leicestershire sergeant and, when two lengths short of them and shaping for a bump, we noticed they were going down hard, by the bows. There was nothing to be done, as the spate was sweeping us quickly downstream and we were completely out of control.

Anyhow, the whole thing was treated as a terrific joke and Love, who was now swimming for it, said he would pick up another boat and catch us up which, sure enough, he did. By about one o'clock we had located the motor boats and soon afterwards we joined up with the others who were safely on board. The sailors, who had been experiencing a perfectly lousy time in the mangrove at the mercy of the mosquitoes, plied us with very welcome rum, cigarettes, sardines and bully beef. It was a fine meal. After this I had a post-mortem with Sandy, on the raid.

The leading car had crashed into the ditch exactly opposite him. The contents of a Tommy gun had been emptied on to the occupants of the back seat and he had identified the badges of rank of the nearest officer as those of a major-general. The total bag of vehicles, accounted for in the ambush, consisted of three staff cars and five lorries. I was disappointed with the results of the raid. In the first place, we had only pulled off one ambush. Secondly, this ambush was nothing to be proud of. The fact that we had bagged a general officer was a pure fluke. We had not got a single identification and this was bad. The surprise effect of our fire must have given us an absolute minimum period of five minutes during which we could have enjoyed complete liberty of action, without any risk whatsoever. The cease fire should have been called after two minutes and then previously detailed men should have gone in to take papers, maps, rank badges and wallets from the dead, whilst other men were detailed to cover them. This would have necessitated no V.C. act of daring. The flanks of the ambush should also have been protected by detachments. What was lacking was 'brains on the job'.

Whilst we sat in the motor boats after lunch, the Malay *serang*, who had produced the *sampans* for Harvey, arrived back, paddling at a good pace with what appeared to be three *coolies*. These turned out to be some privates in the East Surreys whom he had picked up. The poor men were at the limit of their strength. I talked to them and I don't think they realised where they were or what was happening. They addressed me in slow sad, monosyllables saying, for the most part, 'Yes, Sir', or 'I don't know, Sir'. They all carried heavy beards and looked, for all the world, like the pictures of the disciples that I had in my Bible at school. Bill Harvey offered the *serang* a suitable remuneration in return for the lives of these men, but the Malay refused to take it, saying that he had already been more than generously paid. He added that he would always be pleased to help us and that we must let him know if we ever came back. With that he paddled away; a broad grin gleaming from his generous mouth and deep set eyes.

The others seemed pleased enough with our achievements but I sat brooding in the motor boat feeling sullen and despondent. The minutes ticked slowly past. I kept my eyes glued on the mud watching the tide slowly, slowly, ebbing and, at length, after what seemed, hours, noticing the first signs of the flow. We had to stay where we were till the tide put us afloat and, somewhere about 5.30 p.m., we were able to push off. During the afternoon, quite a few Jap aircraft had been overhead, but to find us, in our hideout under the overhanging mangrove branches, was like looking for the proverbial needle. Eventually, we chugged downstream and number two boat again broke down, so we took her in tow. The sun was blanketed by heavy black clouds to the west and, as we came in sight of the sea, darkness fell to the accompaniment of a heavy drizzle which soaked us to the skin.

We were at Point W hours before the appointed time. I shivered as the chill sea breeze cut into my rain-sodden shirt. There had only been enough rum for one shot apiece when we reached the motor boats. I would have liked half a pint of neat rum to cheer me up now.

We waited at Point W during four or five hours of darkness. A Jap plane, with full navigational lights ablaze, flew directly over us at not more than two hundred feet. Eventually, we heard the sound of motor boat engines to westward and flashed the recognition signal; but it was nearly an hour before the craft actually arrived and the noise of the *Fairmile* was equivalent to a bomber squadron.

My launch, 1062, was in company with the *Fairmile*. We tied up alongside. Colonel Warren was standing amidships.

'How did it go?' he said.

'Not too bad, not too good,' I replied.

We talked for a bit and then I said, 'I'm absolutely whacked now, so I'll get aboard 1062. I'll tell you more later'. As a matter of fact, the idea was that all the troops should go back on the *Fairmile* as she was considerably faster. When I was aboard 1062 I found, I was the only one of the raiding party there, but it was too late to change. The skipper gave me a drink and I fell fast asleep on the cabin floor.

When I woke up I found someone's foot was pressed up against my face and at least two other people were using my body as a pillow. I went fast asleep again. The next time I awoke it was just getting light and someone was standing on my head. During the night, the rain had come down in buckets and about a dozen ratings had crowded into the cabin which was about 6 feet 6 inches long by about 6 feet wide. All the same, it seemed luxury to me. Everything is by comparison and war certainly makes one appreciate the comforts of civilization, which one becomes accustomed to take for granted.

I got up leisurely, as soon as the crew had cleared the cabin, and after a shave and a cup of tea felt like a new man. It was a glorious day and I passed the time either on the bridge with the skipper, who was a delightful New Zealander, or in talking to the crew.

We had the two motor boats in tow so our speed was greatly reduced. Furthermore, if this tow was spotted by Jap aircraft we were for the high jump, so we did not take the direct coastal route to Swettenham, but steered a course towards Sumatra and back instead.

About 11 p.m., nearly twenty-four hours after leaving Point W, we tied up alongside *Kudat*. I dragged my body to my cabin and fell into another coma. I dreamed of mangrove swamps that never came to an end, ambushes that wouldn't work out, tracks that petered out in the jungle and compasses that went round in circles; and thus ended the Temerloh Raid.

Chapter 6

Nippon Rules the Waves

After an early breakfast the next morning I decided to go and see
my marines. They had arrived at Swettenham the day that we left and
were training in the local jungle to the best of their ability. On the way
down *Kudat's* gangway I was accosted by the commander of the Australian troops who said that he had been to A.I.F. H.Q. the previous
day and that General Gordon Bennett had sent his congratulations.

On the quayside, I met Colonel Warren and we motored over together to call on the marines who were billeted in some Malay huts.
The 'Bulwarks' were a fine-looking lot of men with smart, well set
up N.C.O.s and commanded by a very young subaltern called Davis.
I liked Davis a lot. He lined up about six foot six inches and had a
side-hat some two or three sizes too small, from which emerged a
crop of unruly hair. He had the heart of a lion and his shy uncertain
manner disappeared completely when there was any danger in the air.
His sense of humour was as constant as his untidiness. Davis asked me
how soon I could lay on a party for his chaps. I said I would initiate
one as soon as possible. It was now December 30th and I promised
to do my best for somewhere about January and, depending a lot on
what the sailors could do.

After the N.C.O.s were introduced to me I drove into Kuala Lumpur, to 3rd Corps H.Q. and was interviewed by General Heath. I
made a very frank report on our raid which was, apparently, in rather marked contrast to the rumours that had been getting around, in
which we were all portrayed as heroes.

The Australians were now planning to do a raid on their own.
P.S.M. Love and Sergeant Skinner had passed through a town called
Taiping, whilst cut off behind the Jap lines. Here they had reported an
aerodrome stiff full of aircraft and a large car-park crammed with vehicles. The Aussies were going to fix up these two installations. I could

not visualise this operation working out in practice, as special equipment and specially trained men would be required for the demolitions and, furthermore, the car-parks certainly and the aerodrome, most probably, would have moved by the time the raid could materialize. However, I left the Australians to work out their own plan as the marines, who were lacking in jungle experience, were particularly anxious that I should accompany them.

There were four main lessons from the Temerloh raid. First, the time spent at sea and the work and strain imposed on the navy were out of proportion to the relatively short time that the soldiers spent ashore. Secondly, the planters, though invaluable as interpreters, lacked the requisite knowledge to act as guides, and guides we definitely wanted. Thirdly, the platoon, unless it was highly trained, was too big a unit for an ambush and better results could be obtained by a larger number of smaller parties working over the same area. Fourthly, there was no difficulty in finding local paddle craft for use in the creeks and, though slow, they were reliable, which is more than could be said for the motor boats. In addition, there were lessons concerning small points of administration such as scales of rations and ammunition.

With these lessons in mind I set about planning another raid which gave every prospect of being a winner. In the first place the navy were going to take us up to a Chinese fishing village called Pasir Hitam, which was not far from Point W. Pasir Hitam was an island with another island between it and the mainland. It could only be approached from the sea, as endless miles of mangrove lay between it and the mainland. We were going to establish an advanced operational base at Pasir Hitam and stay there for ten days. Raiding parties were to go ashore in *sampans*, under cover of darkness, and each party was to consist of only one leader, three men, one native guide and a European interpreter. I got the guides and everything laid on.

I also co-opted the services of an invaluable Scotsman, who had been employed in the anti-smuggling racket at Pasir Hitam before the war. He knew the locals personally and also their habits. Victor Clarke had got some fast Eureka landing craft from Singapore which were due to arrive on January 2nd. One of my guides was a Malayan police sergeant who guaranteed to be able to take me inside three hours by a hill track from Trong to my special place on the Bukit Bubu Pass. The planters, on the previous raid, had estimated the time for the march as nine hours, but they didn't know about the hill track.

I spent most of the next three days between Swettenham and Kuala Lumpur. The marines were short of a lot of equipment and Davies and I spent much time helping ourselves to what we wanted from Ordnance and Supply depots. A brother officer of mine, called Bobby Moir, who was *commandant* of the Federated Malay States Volunteer Forces and commander of the Line of Communication troops, very kindly put me up in his house. His wife, Nellie, was a tower of strength in the local A.R.P. organisation and quite the most public-spirited woman in Malaya. She refused to leave Singapore before it capitulated and was interned by the Japs. Staying with Nellie and Bobbie was always good fun and, even in wartime, this was no exception.

We had an excellent dinner, my first night back, after which I rang up Alison who was more than surprised to hear my voice. I was terribly relieved to hear that she and baby Caroline were to embark at Singapore the next morning. This took a load off my mind which made life a lot easier. You cannot fight when you are looking over your shoulder, and there were too many men in Malaya with an eye to the rear on their wives and families.

Next day I went over early to Swettenham and found the *Kudat* had been sunk in an air attack, so I lost all my kit. On January 3rd, the marines and I were due to embark for Pasir Hitam but disaster overtook us, for on the evening of January 2nd the Japs spotted our Eurekas off the coast, just short of the port. They set about them good and hearty and either sunk or damaged the whole four. Victor said he hoped to get a couple repaired, in which case we could, with luck, leave on January 4th. However, the next day I was summoned to a conference at 3rd Corps H.Q.

We last left the 11th Division behind the Perak River on December 23rd. About this date the Japs started fighting for the crossings at Kuala Kangsar and the pontoon bridge. To fight for a river line, in jungle warfare, is unsound because, although the actual bridges can be held, it is simplicity itself for the attackers to infiltrate to the flanks of crossing places, in the event of an attempt being made by the defence to hold the river as a line. The Perak River was, therefore, by no means the formidable tactical obstacle that it appeared to be on the map. Major-General Paris had now taken over the division. He was quick to see the tactical weakness of the Perak line and decided to withdraw and take up a position at Kampar. Kampar was open tin-mining country where we would get long fields of fire for our automatics and also be able to deploy the whole of our artillery. It was only in this latter arm that we had a superiority over the Japs.

In order to allow time for the Kampar position to be prepared, 12th Brigade was given a delaying role in the area of Gopeng-Dipang. Here Brigadier Stewart fixed up a well thought out counter-attack with his brigade disposed in depth. He issued orders for his leading battalion to withdraw, after contact, so as to let the Japs occupy Gopeng that night. The Nips were very partial to getting under cover and taking their ease at night, and the brigadier hoped they would crowd their troops into this little township. His plan was to make a frontal attack with artillery support early the next morning directed to a depth of two thousand yards through Gopeng. The details of the attack and the artillery barrage were all worked out. Unfortunately, the Japs forestalled this plan by attacking frontally, themselves, against Dipang, with tank support. This attack was met and stopped by 12th Brigade, but it left them sufficiently disorganised to necessitate their own counter-attack having to be called off.

Brigadier Stewart's action at Gopeng-Dipang is a classic example of one of the first principles of jungle warfare; namely, that when the initiative is lost and troops are forced on to the defensive, the battle must be fought 'for the road from the road' and not 'for the road from the jungle'. If Brigadier Stewart had decided to counter-attack by encirclement, he would have been left with insufficient troops on the road, and the Jap frontal attack would have filleted him. As it was, he still retained the road and covered the Kampar position. If there is no road, as in the Arakan at the time of our 1942-43 campaign, this principle does not apply. The main lesson from that campaign is that, unless we were prepared to capture the Arakan from the sea, we should never have embarked on the operation in the first place, except for the purpose of training, and in this case, we should have adopted completely different tactics.

Theorists will disagree with these observations on the ground that the principles of war are firm and established and common to all types of warfare. I contend that in every different type of warfare there are, what I call, different principles, and that it was our failure to appreciate this, and to train specialists, that accounted for the lamentably poor tactical show that we put up *vis-a-vis* the Axis, in the earlier rounds of the present contest. I freely admit that, academically, I may have misused the word 'principle' but it is just that very same academic outlook which, to my mind, was the direct cause of our unsatisfactory standard and performance in the application of our tactics and our strategy.

12th Brigade were withdrawn in due course, through the Kampar position, about December 26th, as far as I know, and then the Kampar battle was joined. The Japs lost dearly in this battle, and all their attacks failed. Our artillery enjoyed some excellent shooting and earned the highest respect from the Japs; which fact was gleaned from captured enemy intelligence summaries. The East Surreys and the Leicesters, who had been amalgamated into one battalion, fought with distinction, as did the Gurkhas. A feature of the fighting was the boldness with which immediate counter-attacks were conducted and the success which attended them.

Having failed to break through the Kampar position the Japs then carried out a major encircling attack, by sea, directed at Telok Anson. Here they were met by the Malayan Independent Company who were reinforced, first by the Argylls, and later by the remainder of 12th Brigade. There was some fierce fighting at Telok Anson which started about January 1st and continued for three or four days. At this battle, European officers were definitely established as being with the forward Japanese troops. It soon became clear that the Japs would be able to overrun our detachment at Telok Anson and, in this eventuality, 11th Division's communications would be cut.

The Kampar position, therefore, had to be abandoned, and a new position selected south of the Bernam River. The position selected was at Slim River and more will be heard of this place later on in the narrative. 12th Brigade covered the left flank of 11th Division in its withdrawal to Slim River and on January 3rd disengaged and executed a skilful retirement to rejoin the division, in the face of the Japanese pincers from Telok Anson and Kampar.

At the conference to which I was summoned on January 3rd, General Heath outlined the most recent developments and said that he anticipated the Japs would now carry out a series of further encircling moves, by sea, directed successively on Kuala Selangor, Port Swettenham, Malacca, and further places to the south. The problem was to find sufficient troops to protect this long and vulnerable left flank. All that was available was Brigadier Moir's Line of Communication Command, which consisted of volunteer detachments. There were about five Federated Malay States Volunteer battalions and three Strait Settlement battalions altogether. Bobby Moir was *commandant* of the former. These battalions consisted of European, Malayan and Chinese companies. The battalions that had not already been disbanded consisted, merely, of detachments, as the Asiatics were given the alternative of handing in their arms or staying, and the majority accepted the first alternative. Bobby Moir had a quite impossible job, and the troops under his command disappeared like melting ice. Consequently, his command varied hourly and his transport and signals were quite unreliable. That he managed to exercise the control that he did was entirely due to his personality, the gift of leadership, which nature had bestowed on him to a very marked extent, and also to the popularity and practical efficiency of his staff.

Bobby, who knew his own men like the back of his hand, had advocated the disbandment of the Volunteers at the G.O.C.'s conference which took place just before hostilities started. He had put up a workable alternative scheme but his proposals were turned down. The Volunteers looked well 'on paper' and they were the jealously guarded property of the Colonial Administration. In war, they were a liability. This organisation locked up a large European element in the guise of simple soldiers, whose services in other capacities could have been invaluable to the army. Desertion in the Volunteers was countenanced and this started a rot which was by no means confined to the Volunteers alone. Once men start moving to the rear, without permission, officers must use their pistols immediately and ruthlessly. If any exceptions are made, panic will set in, and revolver ammunition will soon be exhausted, and to no account either. As a nation, which seems fated to start all wars with reverses, it is as well that this lesson should be absorbed.

At the conference the general said there seemed no doubt that the Japs had got our Commando activities buttoned up and that he must use my troops in an emergency defensive role. In this capacity, it was hardly necessary to retain an officer of my rank for the command of such a small body and so I found myself on the open market. In the first instance my services were borrowed by the commander of one of the Volunteer battalions (who had no confidence in his own military capabilities) in the role of what I can only describe as guide, philosopher and friend. His unit was charged with the defence of Port Swettenham and my Commando troops were kept in hand as a mobile reserve.

On the afternoon of January 3rd, I went round the Volunteers' area and made the necessary dispositions and also co-ordinated the tasks of the local patrol craft to dovetail with this plan. On the following night, I had to dispatch the Commando troops in defensive roles; the marines to Jeram and the Australians to Batu Berjanti bridge. At this latter place the Australians came into action against Japs who had landed north of Kuala Selangor and were infiltrating southwards across the Selangor River. The Australians were relieved on the afternoon of January 5th and reverted to their own H.Q. on the following day, as the special work for which they had been loaned had now terminated.

On January 5th, I had no work to do at Port Swettenham, so I took a holiday and went up to Kuala Selangor in the delightful company of two Gunner officers called Don and Ford. Patrick Don had a troop of his 25-pounder battery at Kuala Selangor and Ford, who was in the same battery, had supported the Australians at Berjanti the previous day. There was a long straight strip of road, short of Kuala Selangor, and the Jap aircraft made a habit of beating up vehicles on this stretch. Bobby Moir gave me permission to go off for my holiday but said he would put me under arrest if I got hit *en route!*

It was very pleasant at Kuala Selangor. There was an old Dutch Fort which overlooked the entrance to the river and on top of this promontory was a lighthouse in which the troop commander had established his O.P. We had a nice lunch and went up to the top of the lighthouse afterwards, from whence we got an excellent view of the surrounding country. In the evening, we returned to Kuala Lumpur where I picked up my car and motored back to Port Swettenham.

I called in at the police station at Klang, on the way back, as I had arranged to impress sufficient bicycles for my marines, through the local police officer. While I was standing outside, a car passed, driving like bats out of hell for Kuala Lumpur. The driver, who was an Indian in the port-authority and a minion of Victor Clarke's, saw me and jammed on all his brakes.

'My God, Major', he said, 'you must get out of this. The Japs have arrived.'

I thought this was nice advice to give an officer, but appreciated his thoughtfulness, all the same. I asked, how, when, and where the Japs had arrived. He said they were arriving now in every conceivable kind of craft. I asked him how many craft he had actually seen. After a bit, more interrogation I found he had seen no Japs and no craft.

'Well, Major, I'll be hurrying along now.'

'All right', I replied, 'but see you don't break your neck.'

When I reached Swettenham, I found everyone sitting in slit trenches, because there had been an air raid earlier on, and no one had taken a jerk on themselves as yet. No battle was in progress so I quite rightly presumed the report I had just received to be an alarmist scare.

Information then came through that the Japs were off Kuala Selangor. This was reliable, as it came over the gunners' wireless from the troop commander. There was one coastal steamer with a tow and some smaller craft. The gunners engaged this target effectively and registered more than one direct hit on the steamer and also damaged some of the craft. The final results were obscured by the gathering darkness but the Jap fleet was forced to withdraw. We celebrated this contest by having some dinner.

After dinner, a fusillade started down on the river. An Asiatic runner appeared in a shocking state of jitters and reported that B Company was engaging a fleet of *tonkangs*, barges and whatnot, that was making its way up the moonlit river. I borrowed a motor-bicycle and rode to the scene of action. I had never heard such a volume of fire in my life, but all I could see on the river was a couple of banana leaves, so I ordered the Cease Fire. It took some time to take effect. The rest of the night passed without incident. We christened this brisk encounter 'The Battle of the Leaves'.

I spent the night in an abandoned Chinese house, the owner of which must have been a salesman in Bata's shoes. This was convenient and I fixed myself up in a pair of 'sneakers' to replace a pair that had gone down in the *Kudat*. It was necessary to have rubber soled shoes so as to be able to move on roads by night with impunity. The next day I was sent for by Bobby Moir and given command of an odd assortment of waif and stray volunteers. Together with my marines, this was to form a special mobile reserve. Anything more immobile would be impossible to imagine. The volunteers were of every nationality and, for the most part, grossly unfit. They knew nothing at all about soldiering, so I started tuning them up right away. We were given huts in a standing camp just outside Kuala Lumpur. First of all, I taught them how to get in and out of vehicles and then I took them on the range and made them fire their weapons. I then taught them how to form an all round defended locality astride a road. This fine body of men, which I am thankful I never had to take into action, was known as Rose's Rifles.

Whilst engrossed in my second day's training, a slightly more corporate body of volunteers, who had their own armoured cars, relieved me in my mobile reserve role and I was told to take the marines off and break up a factory in Kuala Lumpur. This was part of the scorched earth policy which had been instituted in the State of Selangor. The withdrawal in Northern Malaya had taken place at such speed that nothing was destroyed at all, not even the R.A.F. petrol and bomb stores. Incidentally, it was not uncommon to pick up bomb splinters marked G.R. When we were on the inner bridgehead at the Johore causeway we sent some such specimens to the Combined Ops. Room for information! To return, though, to scorched earth. In Selangor, some effort was made to destroy material. The smoke houses were burned down and the ceaseless columns of ascending black smoke from these installations were a familiar feature of the landscape.

To be continually surrounded by monster fires has a most depressing effect; so I found it to be at Kuala Lumpur and subsequently in Singapore. Generally speaking, though, I would describe the results of our destructive activities in Selangor and Negri Sembilan as 'singed earth' at the best. The impression I got from my observations of the civil administration was that it had virtually broken down and was incapable of co-ordinating anything. There were one or two stout-hearted civil servants at work, but the problem was far too big for the existing organisation and there were many insuperable problems to contend with, such as the mass desertion of labour.

The work of smashing up the factory was much to the liking of the marines. Sledge hammers were being wielded with great deftness and we continued with the work till dark that night. On my way back to our billets I dropped off at Bobby Moir's headquarters for a liaison visit. I met Pat Hayward, the brigade major, in the hall and he said, 'I am afraid there's terribly bad news about your regiment. Would you like to go and see Bobby?'

Bobby told me the regiment had been pretty well wiped out that morning, January 7th, at Slim River. Except for that part of the B echelon transport which was not in the battle, only two officers and eighty other ranks had survived. The brigadier and the divisional commander considered the Slim River position to be the strongest that had been taken up in the campaign. Localities had been dug and wired. The Argylls were in depth behind the other two battalions in the brigade. The forward battalion was given liberty to withdraw, after contact, and to step back behind the Argylls. They disengaged, with the brigadier's approval, having reported that the Japs were using medium tanks. Unfortunately, in their withdrawal they took the second battalion with them and it was in this area that the main anti-tank defence was concentrated.

The Jap tank frontal attack hit the Argylls in the early hours of the morning and, at the same time, they were struck in the flank by a powerful encircling attack. Of the few survivors, the majority were from one company which counter-attacked the enemy encircling attack and went through it. None of the runners or patrols, sent forward by Brigadier Stewart, succeeded in getting back and it can only be presumed that the battalion stood to fight on their positions till they were overwhelmed.

The Argylls had made a name for themselves in the fighting in Northern and Central Malaya that will not be lightly forgotten. They had fought the Japs in half a dozen battles and, until Slim River, they reckoned they were killing at least ten to one. They had won the admiration of all those with whom they had come in contact and enriched with honour and glory the traditions of their regiment which had so consistently lived up to its motto, *Sans Peur*. They did not die in vain. Their names will live for ever, and we who fill their vacant ranks must prove ourselves worthy heirs to the reputation of valour, bought at such a price.

The Jap tanks broke through the Slim position and exploited down the road. They ran straight into the 5/14th Punjab Regiment and the 28th Gurkha Brigade who were coming up to relieve the 12th Brigade, and they succeeded in severely disorganising these former troops who were without anti-tank defence.

The Jap tanks looked as if they might get right through to Kuala Lumpur. They were eventually stopped by a British sergeant who, with a crew of three, man-handled a 4.5 How. in the roadway. A 4.5 How. makes a poor anti-tank weapon. There were only four rounds of ammunition with the gun. As the leading tank came round the bend they fired and missed. The second shot registered another miss and, by this time, the entire gun crew, apart from the sergeant, had been killed. The third round, fired at about 75 yards, missed again. The sergeant then reloaded with the last round, waited till the tank was on the muzzle of his gun, pulled the lanyard and knocked it out. For this act of valour, he was awarded the D.C.M.

This story had an interesting sequel. The commander of the Jap tank was a major, and inside his tank he had a leather suitcase which contained, amongst other things, a silver-framed photograph of himself and his wife. This photograph, together with other captured documents, was sent to Divisional Headquarters for information. The Intelligence Branch of the staff was established in Rawang Police Station, and, on the walls, were pictures of all the missing Japs who should have been interned when hostilities started. The photograph of one of them—a bicycle *wallah*—was identical to the one of the Japanese major. Before the war, the country was stiff with Japanese and their activities were allowed to proceed quite unhampered, the main effort of our security police being directed against the Chinese Communist Party.

On January 8th and 9th, the remainder of 11th Division took another mauling and, by this time, the entire division amounted to barely a thousand rifles. Malaya Command required 11th Division to fight in front of Kuala Lumpur till the end of the month, in order that Singapore should be kept out of range of enemy fighter aircraft. A large convoy was due in at the end of the month and, if the Jap bombing formations were given fighter escort, there would be little chance of the convoy escaping destruction at sea. It was however, out of the question for 11th Division to fight again till it was completely re-equipped, reinforced, and reorganised.

A big convoy, containing 99 Hurricanes and the majority of 18th British Division, was due in very shortly and, apart from one big ship (I think it was the *Star of India,* or it may have been the *Empress of Japan*) which was sunk in the fairway, this convoy arrived pretty well intact. The Japs sent a very heavy bombing force to administer the *coup de grace* but, fortunately, a heavy sea fog descended and the bombs fell nowhere near their target. 11th Division had delayed sufficiently long in front of Kuala Lumpur to assist this convoy into port, but they had shot their bolt.

CHAPTER 7

The Retreat to Johore

The withdrawal was due to start on the evening of January 10th. On the 9th I was given a new command called Roseforce, which was to act first as flank guard and then as rear-guard in this withdrawal. The troops under my command consisted of a squadron of 3rd Cavalry (armoured cars), the Malayan Independent Company, a company of Garharwahalis, a carrier platoon from the Dogras, and, last but not least, my trusty and well beloved marines. In addition, I had a battery of 25-pounders and a section of Sappers and Miners in support. My initial area of responsibility was nearly as large as Sussex and I had no staff and no signals. I soon acquired a planter called Mackay to fulfil the duties of second-in-command and adjutant, and also a wireless set to work from my H.Q. to H.Q. L. of C. area.

I spent the whole of January 9th driving round my area, contacting my various subordinate commanders and giving them operational instructions. The best that can be said of my dispositions was that they offered good prospects of a fight before the Japs could do any real damage. All the same, there was virtually no control.

The initial rear-guard was to deny the line Kuala Lumpur—Port Swettenham till dark and then pass through me. I was to take over on the line Kampong Dingkil—Telok Datok—Morib and then to withdraw to the Sepang River.

On the morning of January 10th I was having a telephone conversation, from my headquarters at Telok Datok, with H.Q. L. of C. area, when I heard dive-bombers circling overhead. I was just debating the advisability of ringing off, when I heard the first plane roar down on the bungalow. There was a blinding flash, followed by a deafening explosion and I found myself crumpled up at the far end of the room and the furniture all over the place. Mackay came rushing upstairs

119

calling out, 'Get downstairs, sir, we're in for the hell of a hammering'. Downstairs there were about a dozen marines lying flat on the floor. I had just taken up a horizontal position when the next stick of bombs fell. The door was blown off its hinges and crockery was flying about all over the place. Each successive aircraft gave the impression that it had singled out *you,* personally, and that the next bomb was going to come down slap in the small of your back. I took a look round the marines' faces. Some of them were looking very unhappy, and there were trembling hands and limbs. One boy, who must still have been in his teens, started to whimper, 'I can't stand it—Oh God—I can't stand it'. I felt rather embarrassed and said this was only small stuff and nothing like London and Chatham and Portsmouth had to take in the Blitz. I said, 'You wouldn't like your sister to see you crying, would you?' He steadied up a bit.

Corporal Lilly was lying opposite me. Davis had told me that he had had a close-up of this N. C. O. in action in *Repulse* against the Jap torpedo bombers and that he had been quite magnificent. He was taking this dose all right, with his head up off the floor and looking completely unconcerned. I remember he was in shorts and a singlet, with soap still on his face, having been caught in the middle of a shave. Some of the other men were standing up to it well, which was very creditable after their trying ordeal at sea. Glass was flying about the place and cannon bullets were exploding on the outer walls, I thought it was merely a question of time before we took one direct—and then it all stopped.

Our party was all correct except for some superficial cuts. I went out on the road and found Davis dealing with some of his men who had been wounded. There were a lot of craters on the road and the water main was spouting freely. The bridge was still intact, thank God. Some vehicles, belonging to the Local Defence Corps (who were going back to Singapore) were on fire and blazing merrily. Suddenly there would be a loud detonation as the petrol tank blew up and then the vehicles would settle down into a steady red and yellow blaze. The Independent Company, further up the road, had also suffered some casualties and lost some vehicles. My own car was riddled with machine-gun bullets and was a complete write-off.

I now got the men dispersed and ordered that, in the event of another attack, every single small arms weapon was to fire. This is the best way of maintaining morale and the fact that you don't inflict any visible damage is of no consequence at all. I proved this to my own satisfaction on a number of occasions. Mackay had, by now, raised a new car for me and I drove up to Port Swettenham to contact the commander of the rear-guard from whom I was to take over. He was in contact with the Japs and a stiff action promised to materialise at Batu Tiga. His timings varied from the ones I had been given from L. of C. area but he had no written orders. My wireless had not yet arrived and, as all telephone communication was cut by enemy bombing, I decided to drive across to Kuala Lumpur and see Bobby Moir. When I got to Kuala Lumpur I found most of the bridges already blown and the town evacuated.

Looting had already broken out amongst the Asiatics and, turning into a square, I suddenly found myself in no-man's-land between two opposing sides that were indulging in a brick-batting contest. I had no idea whither H.Q. had moved, and returned to Telok Datok straightaway. The battle at Batu Tiga had started in earnest and an Indian infantry battalion had packed up. The troop commander who had repelled the Jap landing at Kuala Selangor was working as forward observation officer and had his own O.P. up with a company of this unit.

He reported through by W.T.: 'I am afraid it's all up here, the Japs are in and the Indians are laying down their arms. Bring down a concentration on my O.P. and I'll get out in the shemozzle.' And get out he did.

The rear-guard started to come through my position shortly after dark. They reported that the demolition of the railway bridge had failed, so the prospects of a speedy Jap follow up were considerable. Telok Datok bridge was easy to defend, as the river ran in a sharp U with the top pointing to the enemy. I put the marines across the U, with their flanks resting on the river. I had the Dogra carrier platoon covering both arms of the U from the bridge, with one section ready for immediate counter-attack. The remainder of my troops were in depth south of the river.

My orders were that I was not to withdraw till I received instructions from H.Q., as the Dingkil bridge might not be able to stand up to heavy loads and it might be necessary to divert the whole withdrawal by my route. The rear-guard was clear by 10 p.m. My W.T. set had arrived but had still failed to establish communication, by midnight. I had been out of touch with H.Q. since the telephone conversation early that morning, and the prospects were that I should remain so, in which case I must stand at Telok Datok until the last, and only blow the bridge when it was certain to fall into enemy hands. At midnight, I reluctantly sent back my one and only dispatch rider, to try and find H.Q., with a message giving my position and intention and asking for orders. If orders to withdraw did not reach me before 4 a.m., I should not be behind the Sepang before the Jap dive-bombers were at their ruthless mission, and this was to be avoided if possible.

At 2 a.m. I had just given up my dispatch rider for lost when the W.T. set got through to H.Q. We passed a series of messages and I was told to hold on till 0400 hours. This was all right. The moon was now well up and we had a small ambush laid out in front, so I had no anxiety that the bridge would fall into Jap hands. Davis and I were both itching for a Jap reconnaissance clement to blunder into us as we were in a good position to inflict quite a number of casualties with negligible risk to ourselves. Unfortunately, the Japs would not oblige and, at 03:30 hours, I received a message to send my carriers round by Dingkil and then to withdraw.

This was the first bridge I had ever blown and it went up in good style. Funnily enough, I had 'umpired' the blowing of the very same bridge on manoeuvres about three or four weeks previously. In this exercise, I had learned one or two things about demolitions and chief of these was that the sapper who had to blow the bridge didn't know how to work the exploder. I had checked over the demolition early that morning to see that everything was in order and it was just as well that I did, for I found the bridge was armed on the wrong side. Luckily there was time to put this right and also to fill in the numerous craters left by the dive-bombers.

The technique of blowing a bridge is rather obscure. First of all, you write the Sapper in charge an order telling him to blow the bridge at a certain time. In this case the head Sapper was a very efficient *Jemedar* (Viceroy's Commissioned Officer). We sent the bridge-head troops and the demolition party back some 600 yards, whilst the Jemedar explained to me, in Urdu, what he was going to do. I had never attained proficiency in the Hindi language and, although I could speak a little, I could never understand anyone else, so I decided to watch the *Jemedar* and follow suit.

The first thing he did was to draw his pistol, so I drew mine also. I hoped he wasn't going to commit *hari kari,* but I could see no other reason for such a martial act. He then lit a fuse and got off his mark to no ordinary tune. We had not gone very far when a vivid flash turned the night into day. I went flat on my face, on the tarmac, and then a shower of bricks, mortar, and ironmongery hailed all round us. A huge bit of masonry missed my head by a few inches and a smaller missile hit the sole of my boot, cutting the leather, but doing no damage to me.

Speaking fluently in the vernacular, I inquired of the *Jemedar* if this was all in order. This was the actual conversation in which I was most practised, and it goes like this:

'*Teek hai, Jemedar sahib?*'

Jehay, Teek hai sahib.'

Freely interpreted this means:

'O.K. Mr. *Jemedar?*'

'Yes, O.K. Sir.'

We went back to have a look at the damage and both adjudged the results as first class. After that we embussed and drove, in convoy, to the Sepang. I had another bridge to blow, a few miles short of Sepang. This was a wooden one and didn't go up nearly as well as the steel girder bridge at Telok Datok.

In Sepang I met Bobby Moir who told me that the 18th Gaharwahlis had arrived up and taken over rear-guard at Sepang bridge and that Roseforce was to protect the Gaharwahlis' flank and rear. I met the officer commanding the Gaharwahlis down by the river. He said his unit had just arrived out from India and that he knew nothing whatever about this jungle warfare business. He was relieved to hear that I had over two years' almost continuous experience, and, on his suggestion, I made the dispositions for his battalion.

In mobile operations of this nature, the battalion layout consists of a series of company localities, with all round defence, placed astride the main axis of communication. Under the most favourable conditions of defence there will only be one axis, and such was the case in the Gaharwahlis area. In average jungle, a battalion can fight on a depth of a mile and a half to two miles. The conception of presenting a front to the enemy, either in defence or delaying actions, is unsound as, with the abundant natural cover, the enemy will be able to infiltrate through any such position without difficulty. Furthermore, the fields of fire are so restricted that the frontage which any unit can cover is strictly limited and can be easily outflanked. It was failure to appreciate these elementary principles that enabled the Japs to outmanoeuvre us with the greatest ease throughout the Burma campaign. I venture to say that, with commanders of the calibre and experience of General Paris and Brigadier Stewart, the Burma campaign would have been a different story.

When fighting down the road in depth, localities must be successively stepped back, so that Japanese encircling attacks are taken on the shoulder of the defensive layout and not allowed to strike the open road in the rear. The Japs invariably aimed to hit the road in rear of the defensive layout and, if they succeeded, they would put in a road block. We would then have to smash through the road block or else lose all our transport. Smashing road blocks is a particularly difficult manoeuvre, as time is all important and, in Burma, although we had, tanks, we never made much of a success of this particular form of operation, as both commanders and troops were untrained.

The difference between trained and untrained troops, particularly in jungle warfare, is incalculable. Mere numbers are comparatively unimportant. The reinforcements that arrived during the Malaya campaign were not only untrained but also unacclimatised and, although some of them fought gallantly, they did little else except swell the eventual number of prisoners.

This Gaharwahli battalion was, as their commanding officer had already informed me, completely green and, although I had finished my instructions for the battalion layout early in the morning, the troops were not correctly disposed on the ground by nightfall; simply because officers and N.C.O.s did not know how to deploy them. It was not their fault. They had never had the chance of learning.

After completing the Gaharwahlis's layout I then disposed my own unit and sent off Mackay with a couple of lorries to scrounge what he could in the way of petrol, food and ammunition. Normally a unit commander is informed daily of the place where his supplies and ammunition are to be collected, but things were too disorganised to rely on this information coming through. Incidentally, I received a message after dark, that night, to say that my petrol and supply points would open at Rantau at 1200 hours and close at 1500 hours that same day; so, I was glad that I had sent Mackay off on the scrounge without waiting for instructions.

As it was unlikely that Roseforce would be in action before the Gaharwahlis had been contacted frontally, I decided in favour of indulging in some heavy ablutionary work; more especially as there was a sandy-bedded stream near my H.Q. Thither I repaired about noon with all my toilet necessaries and, having attended initially to beard and teeth, I stripped naked and sat immersed, with the clear, cool water rolling soothingly over my shoulders and the nape of my neck. After lathering and scrubbing activities were completed I felt inspired to recline on a mossy stone, with my feet in the water, and manicure my nails.

When I eventually rejoined my soldiery I was in King's Birthday parade order and feeling like a million dollars. My potential fighting value was increased out of all proportion to the effort involved, and thus the basic fact emerges that, if a man does not take every opportunity to attend to his outward and visible graces, he loses his inward and spiritual soul; and it is the latter quality that counts in war. This applies not only to bodily cleanliness but to all other forms of smartness, whether individual or regimented; hence the paramount importance of insisting on first class parade-ground drill as forming a vital part in the syllabus of training troops for war.

That night, after supper, I took Mackay with me to visit the Gaharwahlis. We went down the road without meeting a sausage, till we found ourselves up against the demolished Sepang bridge. I said that this was unfortunate as we would probably get shot up by our own side on the way back. We stalked back and eventually picked up a company locality. For all they knew we might have been Japs and it would have been very easy meat for half a dozen determined men to scatter these troops to the four winds, as they were completely off their guard. We then disclosed our identity and got a guide to take us up to battalion headquarters.

Here I pointed out to the C.O. that unless the men were formed into close night perimeter within their localities, they stood a very fair chance of being overrun during darkness. The C.O. issued orders accordingly and, in due course, we took our leave. The guide that took us back lost his way and we finished up again at the Sepang bridge. This time I was certain we would get shot up; but not at all. The troops were in exactly the same state of total unpreparedness. On returning to my headquarters, which was in the marines' locality, things were quite different. We were brought to a halt with one bayonet at the throat and another in the small of the back.

The next morning the Gunners took a shoot on the far bank of the Sepang River, where a small party of Japs was reported. I changed my tactical layout after breakfast and we took a couple of severe dive-bombing attacks before lunch. Contact could be expected at any moment and I had a very nice ambush teed up at a place where I expected any Jap encircling attack, initiated at the Sepang river, would strike our main axis. Unfortunately, though, the Japs did not come on.

Withdrawal orders arrived in the afternoon. The Gaharwahlis were to pass through me. I was to take over rear-guard again, blow another couple of bridges and then go into reserve at Malacca. About tea time Mackay returned from one of his scrounging expeditions, with the alarming report that, while at Port Dickson, he had seen a boat, with tow, making for the beach. I cross-questioned him at length and he was certain of his facts. This was disquieting news, as it probably meant that the Japs were to put a road block across my line of withdrawal. I sent a message to Bobby Moir and informed him that I was dispatching a detachment from the Malayan Independent Company to deal with the situation. At dusk Pat Hayward, the brigade major, arrived and said the reported landing was nothing more than a wreck which had been lying off Port Dickson for several days. He pulled my leg mercilessly about raising wind-up rumours, and I had a few words to say myself, on the same subject, to my informant.

Pat Hayward announced his intention of joining up with my rear-guard and invited me to dine with him, in the Port Dickson Club, at midnight. Pat had an excellent sense of humour which he retained through every minute of that depressing retreat. He said, 'It doesn't matter if we are a bit late for dinner as the servants have already given notice and left, and you needn't bother to change as it will be quite an informal evening'.

Darkness fell and with it came the rain. The transport company which was to pick up the Gaharwahlis ground its way slowly forward and, after what seemed hours, the lights of the leading vehicle could be seen returning. We used full headlights in all our withdrawals and it was only in the back areas that blackout lighting on vehicles was observed. The Gaharwahlis reported themselves clear and that was the last I saw of this doomed unit. They were well-nigh annihilated a few days later at Muar, Colonel Wilberforce, the commanding officer, losing his life.

Guides were at Malacca to meet my units and conduct them to their billets. Pat Hayward and I drove with two carriers at the rear of the column and, about midnight, we stopped to blow a bridge just outside Port Dickson. With this obstacle between ourselves and the Japs, we repaired to the club where Pat had laid on a most sumptuous repast including caviar. After dinner, we lolled about on sofas, talking and smoking cigars. Pat was keen that, when we got back to Singapore, he and I should take a party upcountry and establish ourselves on Kedah Peak where he said we could hold out indefinitely. After my recent seafaring experiences, I very much doubted if we would ever get to this place, but I daresay it could have been done by crossing first to Sumatra. Even then it would have been an enormous undertaking to bring all our requirements in supplies, so I told Pat that I did not support his scheme. We then continued with our bridge blowing motor drive, till dawn found us at Malacca.

I disliked that day in Malacca more than any other in the whole war. Everything seemed to go wrong. First, I was unable to find any of my sub-units, so I eventually went to the Rest House for a wash and a shave. Here I found Bobby Moir's gold pencil on a table and, after that, General Heath's A.D.C. making tea in the kitchen. This was all right, as I liked Humphrey, the A.D.C., very much and there was nothing I wanted more than a cup of tea. The general joined us out on the veranda and we bucked away for quite a time. It was quite remarkable how the general always seemed to have time to talk to junior officers like myself. He liked us to talk openly and express our views. He knew us all by name and most of us by our Christian names and his kindly smile and quiet unruffled manner, at a time when the dice were so heavily loaded against him, fully merited the affection and admiration which we all held for him. His example was an inspiration to us all in those days of darkness.

After breakfast an old man of semi-Asiatic extraction, together with a girl of about nineteen whom I took for his grand-daughter, appeared with tears in his eyes and asked for our compassionate assistance. The old boy had a Sunbeam motorcar of incredibly ancient vintage which had died on him and, since the civil administration had packed up, he was stranded. I told the general I would try and have them evacuated, and drove them both to the Casualty Clearing Station. However, there I was informed that they already had more sick and wounded than they could deal with, so I was left in the embarrassing position of having to incorporate these two non-combatants into Roseforce.

On my way, back from the C.C.S., dive-bombers appeared on the scene, so I pulled up and told my refugees to get out and into a slit trench. There was no slit trench and, at that moment, down screamed a bomber and dropped an egg pretty close. The girl got a splinter in her thigh and the old boy was cut a bit by glass. Neither was seriously wounded, and this was absolutely splendid, as now they would have to be accepted by the C.C.S. I washed the old boy down with my water bottle and bound up the girl with my first-field dressing, and there we waited for a motorcar to arrive, as mine had been written off by the bomb.

I was relieved to have these two taken off my hands but, now that my car was out of action, I was completely immobile. I started, on foot, to search for my sub-units. Everywhere I went I got dive-bombed, the worst experience being at Malacca Bridge where a Sapper lorry, full of gelignite, got a direct hit. It made a terrible mess and a large number of men were killed. I frankly admit that this experience shook my nerve and I was in very poor order for two or three hours afterwards. I eventually contacted the Independent Company and acquired a new motor car. This came from a rather unexpected source, a Jock soldier in the company giving me one which he explained he 'didn't particularly want'. The body bore a certain resemblance to a pepper caster, but the engine was excellent and it carried me back to Singapore. Later on, I gave it to my commanding officer; so much for the spoils of war.

After finding my other sub-units I went up to Bobby Moir's H.Q. where I had a bath, shave, and lunch. Half an hour of Pat Hayward's company restored my morale to normal and we then received further orders.

11th Division, which included the L. of C. troops, was to withdraw, during the night January 13-14th, through the next line of resistance which was organised in Johore. 11th Division were withdrawn on three parallel routes, all of which emerged into one bottle-neck at Segamat. There was no co-ordinated movement table and there could not very well have been one, as nobody had the faintest idea of the number of vehicles in the various units of the formation. Our route of withdrawal was down the coast road to the ferry at Muar, and then back again, in a north-easterly direction, towards the main road. The central column tapped in on our route at Tangkak and we eventually joined the left column at Segamat. One thing was dead certain and that was that there would be a first rate 'bog-up' on the road that night. Roseforce was to lead off in the van and we were timed to pass the starting point at 1800 hours. Once through the Johore line, my various sub-units were all detailed to rejoin their parent units, so Roseforce would become defunct.

The first part of the withdrawal went very well. We did a steady 20 m.p.h. and reached Tangkak before 2100 hours. Here we were held up for a long time while vehicles of the central column went past. At 2200 hours, we were let forward by the traffic control, and Mackay laid a bet with me that we would clear the 34 miles to Segamat by midnight. I took the bet for 5 bucks and laid him another 5 that we wouldn't be clear by 0600 hours the next morning. Checks started getting serious after about ten miles. In another few miles, we were progressing in rapidly decreasing bounds of a few hundred yards and then God's own mess set in. A regiment of artillery, coming up the road, met our convoy going down. Double banking started and no sooner had one jam been sorted out than another started. When the column halted, the drivers, drunk with fatigue and exhausted from lack of sleep, fell unconscious over their wheels.

Officers were moving up and down the columns shaking up sleeping drivers, cursing at those that cut-in and collecting what dispatch riders could be found to pass orders up and down the column. In spite of all this, the columns progressed so slowly that movement virtually ceased. The prospects for the following dawn were unpleasant. We would be at the complete mercy of the dive-bombers and the whole road would soon be one blaze of burning vehicles. All we should be able to do would be to bring every weapon that we had into action, but this would not save the vehicles. Eventually, to clear the roads, vehicles had to be slung off into the ditches.

I had already won the first leg of my bet and, with the first streaks of dawn, we were still short of Segamat, and this completed my double. With the aid of daylight, matters improved somewhat. I went on and checked all my vehicles past. They had got badly mixed up with transport of other units and it took some time before they were all through. I was entertained in my vigil by an Australian traffic control man. He explained to me, at some length, just how they were going to fix up the Japs in Johore. I listened patiently and hoped he was right in his forecast.

As we had not slept for four nights, I decided to harbour the marines for the day in a large coconut estate just south of Labis. I also did not fancy using the main road in daylight as the Jap dive-bombers would be giving it their close attention. If the Jap had been able to use his air arm effectively at night, he could have played havoc with our big strategic withdrawals. We had a badly needed rest in the coconut estate that day. I called on the manager who had a most comfortable bungalow. He gave Mackay and me a very welcome bath after which we had a sleep and then some lunch. In the afternoon, I said goodbye to the marines, who were bound for the naval base, and Mackay and I set off for Singapore.

The roads were flooded and we got stuck in quite a few places with water well over our exhaust. I found the best way of dealing with these stoppages was to get a lorry or other high-clearance vehicle to drive into one from behind and push the car out.

We arrived safely in Singapore about dusk. I dropped Mackay at a Chummery where he had friends and thanked him for his very valuable assistance, in return for which he paid me my ten bucks and said I had taught him more about soldiering in five days than he had learnt in the last twenty, as a volunteer.

CHAPTER 8

Interlude in Singapore

It was a strange feeling suddenly to find oneself with no command and no responsibility and, although I had only notched a total of about six hours' sleep in the last four days, my present circumstances produced a sensation of terrific exhilaration. The Millers had very kindly offered me a home, if ever I should be in need of one, so I moved round to their house, after looking in on the Selby-Walkers for a quick one *en route*. We set about celebrating my return by organising an impromptu party, which was a roaring success. On my way home, in the early hours of the morning, I ran across a few soldiers looking for a lift, so I stopped and asked them where they wanted to go. It turned out that they were Argylls, so we crammed the car up to the roof and headed for Tyersall.

'We hear you're coming back to take command of the battalion, Surr,' said one of the Jocks.

'Aye, shure enough, the major's for the command,' added another.

I said this was the first I'd heard of it, but I hoped it was true.

'And look you, Surr', said another, 'there's plenty stoories of draftin' ither bodies to the regiment an' w' dinna want ony o' that. We'll jist stay Argylls and niver heed if there's nae sa mony of us.'

The next morning I went up to Tyersall expecting to find Ian Stewart in the brigade office and I was more than surprised to find Archie Paris back in his old chair with brigadier's badges of rank. Ian Stewart, in his turn, was back in command of the battalion. Now that 11th Division was out of the line to reorganise and refit, it had been appreciated that an Indian Army officer was best suited for command and Brigadier Key had been selected for this appointment, in place of General Paris who was British Service. This reversion to former rank was no reflection on the ability of either Brigadier Paris or Colonel

Stewart. 12th Brigade was now taken out of 11th Division and reverted to its original reserve role. Brigadier Paris told me that he had asked for me to come back to the regiment to command but, now that everyone had gone down a place, he would have to make a renewed application.

The same morning I discovered, through a chance meeting with a staff officer in a hairdresser's shop, that I had been selected as G.S.O.2 Operations, Singapore Fortress. This job was deeply embedded in concrete and not at all to my liking, so I immediately set about the delicate task of oiling out of it. In this I received every support from the brigadier and my commanding officer and, in anticipation of posting orders, I attached myself unofficially to the regiment and gave Fortress Headquarters as wide a berth as possible. After about a fortnight, official notification came through that I would relinquish my staff appointment and revert to regimental employment.

The total strength of the battalion, on arrival at Singapore, was five officers and one hundred and thirty-five other ranks. We took everyone, on whom we could lay our hands, out of extra-regimental employment and, together with some of the earlier wounded who had been discharged from hospital, we raised a total of about two hundred and fifty all ranks. These we organised into two very weak rifle companies of about eighty strong and a very modified battalion headquarters and headquarter company. The latter consisted of a section of mortars, a strong armoured car platoon and a bare minimum of Signallers.

Our armoured car platoon had been the backbone of the battalion and had accounted for a very large number of Japanese. The vehicles with which we were equipped were very ancient Lanchesters which I remember seeing on Salisbury Plain in 1935 when they were the property of the 12th Lancers. They had been sent out to Malaya as training vehicles, but Ian Stewart was quick to perceive their potential tactical value, compared with carriers, and soon had the whole boiling on the unit establishment. These were the heaviest armoured vehicles that we possessed in Malaya. There were no tanks, as our Higher Command had not considered tanks suitable for jungle warfare. The Japs, on the other hand, used them with decisive success.

We had a large number of carriers, which proved themselves absolute death-traps, and also some lightly armoured Marmon-Harrington cars, which were not much better. I remember, before the war started, the official photographer in Singapore (who incidentally was reputed to have been a Japanese officer) expressing his opinion, on the occasion of photographing our transport, that carriers would be useless in jungle warfare as it would be easy to drop grenades and shoot into them from trees. This turned out to be sound advice and a correct forecast.

We started training officers and N.C.O.s with as little delay as possible and, with this end in view, I instituted a regimental *cadre*. Every effort was made within the battalion to keep the men fully occupied and amused. This was no easy matter with a deficiency of experienced officers and N.C.O.s as, apart from this aspect of unit welfare, there were a lot of administrative problems to overcome. In the evenings, there were films and impromptu entertainments and also a limited amount of leave into the town for both officers and rank and file. When my turn came round for the latter privilege I took good care to see that as much fun was to be had as possible and I do not recollect any occasion on which I failed in my object.

I dare say it was frolics such as these that accounted for certain stories which got around, to the effect that Singapore fell on pink gins and parties. This was an entirely unwarranted criticism. The Higher Commands and their staffs were abstemious, quiet, and conventional. If they were open to criticism in some respects, there was certainly not the vestige of evidence for a charge of light-headedness or exuberance of spirits. The predominant atmosphere was one of gloom and despondency which a few of us did our best to eliminate with the object of raising morale and enjoying what little was left of our apparently doomed lives.

No sooner had we arrived back in Singapore than the Japs started daylight air raids which became a regular routine feature of life. These raids were carried out at high altitude by formations, usually, of twenty-seven aircraft. The leader of the formation would give the signal for bomb release and all aircraft would drop their sticks simultaneously. This would result in the matter of perhaps a couple of hundred bombs landing almost simultaneously in a comparatively small area. The targets usually selected were the docks, naval base or base installations, but sometimes the residential areas would be singled out. This form of attack we designated as the 'diarrhoea' type, to differentiate from the 'dive-bombing' variety. To be caught inside the pattern area of a 'diarrhoea' attack was distinctly unpleasant, as the noise was devastating and the blast and splinter effect considerable.

The advantage of this type over the dive-bombing form was that it was soon finished. The first indication of trouble was the peculiar rumbling sound of aircraft in the distance. After a measure of time, the ack-ack would open up and the white puffs of 3.7 shells would give an indication as to the whereabouts of the aircraft. They might or might not be heading in your own particular direction. If they were not, it was usual to take up a suitable position and comment on the ack-ack performance.

Generally, the shooting was excellent and it was not uncommon to see an enemy bomber destroyed by a shell. It was very heartening to see the Jap planes taking punishment and on sonic occasions, when I noticed formations changing course, I fancied our gunners had forced them to deviate from their original objectives. If the formation headed in one's direction it was advisable to move to the proximity of a slit trench. If one's own area was a target for attack the bombs would start whistling when the aircraft were overhead. This was the signal to drop with deliberation but dignity into a trench and assume an eastern praying posture.

The difficulty, after these raids, was to get men out of their trenches immediately and to continue work or normal activity without delay. There was nothing worse for morale than excessive recourse to the slit trench. People who spent longer than necessary in trenches were known as 'cave-dwellers' and to be designated a 'cave-dweller' was tantamount to an insult. The term 'cave-dweller' originated from some cheap publicity photographs of Tobruk which had recently appeared in the illustrated papers. There were three types of cave-dwellers; 'casual', 'deliberate', and 'Lord God Almighty'. The qualification necessary for the last-named type was for a man, who had never previously been known to work after lunch, to be seen digging a slit trench for himself in the heat of the afternoon. 'Deliberate' dwellers established themselves permanently in trenches with their essential requirements in kit and stores, one item of which would undoubtedly be a bottle of whisky, whilst 'casual' dwellers merely took to ground rather earlier than necessary.

About ten days after our arrival back in Singapore my cousin, Mike Bardwell, suddenly appeared in the mess one morning clad in a pair of plimsoll shoes, a ragged shirt, and a pair of well-holed shorts. He had survived the action at Slim River and, in company with one or two others, had made his way to the coast at Jeram. Here the party had bought a *junk* off the local Chinese and sailed to Sumatra. P.S.M. Colville, our pioneer sergeant, a most versatile soldier and entertaining companion, had been an invaluable acquisition to the party, and it was largely due to him that the navigation was so successfully accomplished. Mike had bad jungle sores on his bare legs, and his hands were raw from excessive peeling of yam potatoes, but he was in excellent heart otherwise and told me how he had succeeded in obtaining an air passage to Singapore. We were all delighted to see him back and hear his experiences, but no one more than his pretty little *fiancée*, Kate Londun, who came up to join in the small celebration which we staged for the occasion.

CHAPTER 9

The Withdrawal from Johore

Whilst our training was progressing in Singapore, events were not going any better on the mainland. After 11th Division disengaged, north of Kuala Lumpur, the next defence was organised on the general line Endau—Mersing, Gemas—Labis, Muar—Batu Pahat. The troops to fight on this line consisted of the A.I.F., part of the 9th Indian Division and one brigade of the newly arrived 18th Division. 9th Division consisted of the two brigades initially disposed at Kota Bahru and Kuantan, and had been further reinforced by 45th Indian Infantry Brigade, freshly arrived from India.

There was, of course, no continuous line of defences across the 120 odd miles stretch of country, between the cast and west coast. In the first place, several army corps would have been required to man any such line and, moreover, about a year's intensive work would have been necessary to prepare and organise the detailed dispositions. Even had a position of this nature been in existence, its flanks could have been turned, once the Japs had command of the sea, and this is my answer to critics who suggest that our correct strategy should have been to limit our defence scheme to a 'Johore Line'. It would, I think, have been possible to hold Singapore, provided several additional millions had been spent on turning the island into a fortress. This would have entailed clearing and reclaiming all the mangrove swamps and virtually putting the whole island into concrete.

Concrete cover would also need to have been provided for the odd three quarters of a million Asiatic civilians, and the work and expense entailed would have been prodigious and lengthy. On the military side, the weakness of this policy was that the defence of Singapore would have been essentially passive and that the naval base could not have been used, as it would be automatically neutralized by enemy forces on the northern side of the Johore Strait. Under such conditions, it is hard to see how Singapore could have ever been relieved or fulfil its function as a pivot of manoeuvre in the south-west Pacific.

The only alternative, therefore, was the forward policy of holding the whole peninsula and here, I think, our strategy was quite correct. The fault lay in the fact that we made inadequate provision, in aircraft and crews and in men and material, for implementing our policy. This omission, though, must be considered in the light of our entire Imperial commitments at the time. It is debatable whether or not our forward policy should have included an advance into Thailand and, with inadequate knowledge of the factors at issue, I am not prepared to criticize. My personal view is that the Japs expected and wanted us to cross the frontier and advance on Singora and that, had we done this, 11th Division would have been annihilated by about December 12th.

To revert now to the so-called Johore line. The troops were disposed in depth on the three main axes of possible advance; that is to say, the Endau River and the Mersing beaches in the east; the main trunk road and railway in the central bottle-neck between Gemas and Labis; and, on the western seaboard, the coast between Muar and Batu Pahat, from whence communications ran inland that could be used by the enemy for encircling our dispositions in the central bottle-neck.

My information about the fighting in Johore was all gathered from narratives gleaned from various officers whom I met at conferences and so forth, during the later stages of the campaign as, since I was now at regimental duty, I had no access to the War Diaries and Situation Reports of Higher Headquarters. I trust that the following account is moderately accurate and apologize in anticipation of possible errors.

The Jap follow-up after the North Malayan fighting was extremely quick, and contact was made, on the central route at Gemas, about January 15th. At Gemas, the Australians had laid on a well-planned ambush. A bridge was blown, with another one well to the enemy's rear prepared for demolition. The Japs were to be allowed to pile up on the road behind the first demolition and, when sufficient were in the bag, the second bridge was to be blown. At the same time, an Australian battalion was concealed in the jungle, to the flank of this strip of road, and the blowing up of the second bridge was the signal for this unit to attack and annihilate everything on the road. Trees on the roadside had already been prepared for demolition, so that enemy armoured vehicles would be immobilised. The ambush was entirely successful. The Aussies attacked with great *elan* and estimated that they killed about a thousand Japs against a loss to themselves of a hundred killed and wounded. In conjunction with this ambush, our newly arrived Hurricanes went into action and took great toll of the enemy transport, which was piled up at very close density for many miles in rear.

The recent shipment of Hurricanes were now going into action piecemeal, as quickly as they could be assembled. They rendered a very good account of themselves, both against the high-level bombing attacks on Singapore and also in close support of the Australians. Nevertheless, they were gradually overpowered and eventually eliminated by the early days of the fighting in Singapore island. The Aussies were the only troops in the Malayan campaign to fight with any measure of air support and for this small mercy may they be truly grateful.

After taking a bloody nose at Gemas, the Japs had recourse to their usual encircling tactics and started to infiltrate by sea into the Muar—Batu Pahat area. They put up an effective road block behind the 45th Indian Infantry Brigade and Gordon Bennett dispatched his 19th and 29th battalions to attack the Japanese rear and relieve 45th Brigade. They were unsuccessful in this operation and were eventually re-encircled themselves by fresh Japanese forces. As a result of this, they were ordered to fight back to the main axis of communication at Yong Pen. Several days of what was probably the bitterest fighting in the campaign now ensued.

The Aussies, in spite of a spirited effort, were unable to clear the Jap road block and, eventually, were forced to abandon and destroy their vehicles and regain their own lines by way of the jungle. In this battle the wounded had a bad time. Permission was requested from the Japs for ambulances to be allowed a free passage through the road block. The Japs, quite understandably, refused this request, except on the terms of unconditional surrender. Furthermore, they retained an ambulance as an integral part of their road block. The driver of this vehicle, displaying considerable gallantry and resource, released the handbrake during the night and regained his own lines.

About the time that the Bukit Payong battle was drawing to a close, the Japs instituted a further encircling move in the Batu Pahat area, and the Norfolk and Cambridge Brigade, which had already been in action on the central road, was deviated to deal with these landings. I have no knowledge of how the fighting went, but the Japs succeeded in cutting them off and the Loyals, who had been detached from Singapore Fortress, were unable to extricate them by a counter-attack. My experience of counter-attacks in this campaign was that, between the time they were planned and the time they could be launched, the situation had deteriorated to such an extent that the actual conditions prevailing never gave the faintest prospect of success. In consequence, they either had to be called off or put into effect as mere suicide efforts. Immediate counter-attacks, led by the local commander on the spot and planned from the information he received with his own eyes or ears were a different matter; but for deliberate counter-attacks to succeed it was usually necessary to disengage, completely, and to fight on previously selected ground. This entailed sacrificing the existing situation. The Gemas action serves as a good example of a successful deliberate counter-attack.

The troops cut off in the Batu Pahat area, which consisted of elements of 9th Indian Division, in addition to the Brigade of 18th Division, had, eventually, to destroy their transport and stores, and be evacuated by sea. This difficult operation was skilfully effected by the Royal Navy. I had the greatest admiration for the sailors all through the campaign. They were a most cheerful and willing lot of chaps with whom to work and, when they had lost their ships, were prepared to take on anything in the way of a job, from driving railway trains to full-blooded soldiering. This was in marked contrast to the spirit of the R.A.F. ground staffs who, once their aircraft were destroyed, had one idea only, and that was to get out of it as quick as they could and save their precious bodies for another day. In theory, this was quite sound but in practice the departure was too often unduly accelerated, and achieved only at the expense of abandoning valuable stores and papers.

The situation at Batu Pahat put our dispositions in Johore on a very delicate footing and things were not improved when, towards the end of the month, a Japanese convoy was sighted off Endau.

I was out on training with my *cadre* one afternoon when we saw a formation of our own aircraft heading northwards. There was some speculation amongst the Jocks as to what type of aircraft these could be. One of them thought they were Flying Fortresses, but, in point of fact, they were antiquated old Wildebeestes plugging slowly through the air on their way to bomb the Endau convoy. I believe none of these aircraft returned. It was tough luck on our pilots to have to fight under conditions amounting to little less than suicide. The courage of the men that flew these machines, was epic.

An appreciation of the situation in Johore led Malaya Command to decide that we must now abandon the peninsula and withstand a siege in Singapore. There was now, obviously, no other course open. The plan for the withdrawal was simple. An outer bridgehead, on the Johore causeway, was to be formed by withdrawing one battalion from each of the detachments on the three main axes of communication; that is to say the east, central, and west coast roads. There was to be an inner bridgehead in the immediate vicinity of the causeway, whose main task was to prevent any Japanese infiltrated troops from establishing themselves in a position whence they could bring fire to bear on the causeway and the routes leading to it.

The main bodies were to pass through the outer bridgehead on the night of January 30-31st. The outer bridgehead was to delay the enemy till daylight, or a few hours afterwards if necessary, and then pass through the inner bridgehead. The inner bridgehead was to fight, if necessary, till the last man and the last round. The Argylls had the honour of being selected to hold the inner bridgehead. Colonel Stewart was to command the troops on the two bridgeheads and I assumed command of the Argylls.

There was a commanders' conference at Johore Bahru on the 27th and another on the following day and, at these, we were given our orders and the details of the plans. By this time, Johore Bahru had been selected as a pattern bombing target and conferences were apt to be interrupted by the approaching rumble of high-flying formations, which would subsequently deposit their loads either on or near us.

At one of these conferences I had the privilege of meeting Lieut.-Colonel Anderson who had commanded one of the two Australian battalions at the Bukit-Payon battle. At that time, I did not know he was, shortly, to be the recipient of the Victoria Cross for his inspired leadership and personal courage. He bore no traces of his recent ordeal and talked in a charming and pleasantly unassuming manner. Behind his kindly eyes, though, he radiated a spirit of calculated confidence. 'You'll find your boys will be all right on the inner bridgehead,' he said. 'The Japs don't come on a great deal.'

Here I think he was quite right. Both in Malaya and Burma the Jap tactics were to establish a road block in our rear and then put the onus of a frontal attack on us. Their stalker snipers, or shock troops, who were normally disguised as local natives and lightly armed and equipped, would sneak through our forward troops and then make as much noise as they could, to give the impression that they were in much greater strength, than was the case. At Jitra, Kota Bahru and Kampar, where the Japs did make frontal attacks, they came on all right, regardless of casualties, but I think it is safe to say that, generally speaking, they would prefer to gain the initiative, establish themselves in our rear and then force us to attack. With well-trained troops, we should have been able to defeat these tactics, as Colonel Stewart did at Kota Tampan, which was the only occasion on which the Japs managed to seize the road in rear of the 12th Brigade.

Colonel Anderson's personality left a very marked impression on me. A namesake of his, Andy Anderson of the 15th Punjabis, who had been at the Staff College with me, was killed whilst acting as liaison officer to the Australians at Bukit Payon. By all accounts he put up a most spirited performance over many days and nights and his gallantry will rank high in the deeds of the Malayan Campaign.

By the afternoon of January 28th, I had completed my reconnaissance and decided on my dispositions. I returned to Tyersall and gave orders for the move to the causeway the following morning. When sufficient time was available, I used to dictate my orders to my adjutant who would have them typed and then distribute copies to my officers when they were assembled. I then gave out the orders verbally, allowed a minute or two for thought, and concluded with 'Any questions?' My orders never took more than a few minutes, and recipients left with a clear idea of their duties.

I think it should be a golden rule never to have a conference. If you want anyone's opinion or advice, then ask him what you want to know. Conferences lead to indecision and most often culminate in confused and complicated orders which break down under the strain of battle conditions. Orders must be short and simple. The more thorough the training of a unit has been the more manoeuvres will it be capable of executing, but simplicity of plan and orders is still paramount. With untrained troops (like Rose's Rifles) no tactical movement whatever is possible. When I took over this fine body of men I said to Bobby Moir, 'What kind of tactics do you think we might employ;'

'Oh,' said Bobby, 'just simple stuff.'

It took me the best part of half an hour to get them formed up into platoons. This shows the difference between trained and untrained troops.

We moved out of Tyersall on the 29th. I went on ahead and met my company commanders in the main square, north of the causeway, where I gave out orders for the occupation of the position. The troops

141

arrived, debussed and deployed. Work had hardly started before the ominous drone of bombers headed in our direction and a few minutes later we found ourselves the victims of a diarrhoea attack. I was right out in the open when the whistling started and decided in favour of a small fold in the ground rather than the communal protection of an already overcrowded shelter. After these high-level attacks, it was vital for officers to get men on to their feet straight away and to make a search for any cave-dwellers. It also heartened the warriors if the officers drove round and showed themselves, taking a chat with the odd man here and there.

There was a lot of work to be done on the position, including the siting and digging of weapon slits and alternative positions, clearing fields of fire, putting buildings into a state of defence and checking the fire effect of individual weapons. We were not given any wire as it was all required on the island. This work went on all through the 29th and 30th.

On the morning of the 30th I laid on the artillery defensive fire tasks with an Australian Gunner officer. We had two whole artillery regiments, a total of forty-eight guns, in support of us. Apart from the defensive fire tasks we also planned the prophylactic fire that would be brought down on our own actual positions, in the event of our being ordered to withdraw from close contact.

At 11 o'clock I gave out verbal orders for the withdrawal on the following morning. 1100 hours was about the time that the Japs put over their second high-level attack and I selected a large slit trench as the rendezvous for my orders group. No sooner had we all assembled than the bombers announced their presence. This time we were right in the middle of the pattern area. We had a very near miss on our trench which, fortunately, turned out to be a dud. Whether it was a dud or an un-exploded bomb I never discovered. There were several of the latter in our area, one of which had cratered the road in the middle of our dispositions. I drove past this one several times during the day, in an armoured car, in blissful ignorance that the weight of the vehicle on the tarmac might easily detonate the bomb. It was in this attack that I picked up a fair-sized splinter marked G VI R.

I had always wanted to write a special order of the day and, as this was my first and quite probably my last opportunity, I decided not to let the chance slip. The order as far as I remember, read like this:

'The task which has been allotted to the battalion in the defence of the inner bridgehead on the Johore Causeway, is vital to the success of future operations on the Island. Enemy action, whether by ground or air, will be resisted to the maximum of human endurance, which has no limit.'

The Jocks liked this one and there was considerable demand on Corporal Masterton, the Orderly Room Sergeant, for extra, copies.

In the evening, I carried out a final inspection of the whole position and, after this, I conducted two full dress rehearsals of the withdrawal, so that in the heat of action every man would know instinctively what was required of him. This concluded a fairly busy day. Sentries were posted and we stood down for the night.

My headquarters were in a comfortable house, perched on a steep escarpment overlooking the Johore Straits. We had a Frigidaire in the house and some soda and beer on the ice. Mike Bardwell, who was on sick leave, had been married to Kate that afternoon and thoughtfully sent up a couple of bottles of champagne and some wedding cake with the B echelon transport, but, unfortunately, these wedding comforts never found their way as far as my H.Q. We had a very good dinner at my residence that night and concluded it by concocting a bogus letter, purporting to come from General Percival and addressed to General Heath. In this letter, we referred to a new secret weapon and also an intended landing by a fictitious Guards Division at either Endau or Port Swettenham. This we left on the dinner table, together with our unwashed plates, for the enlightenment of the Japanese Intelligence Staff!

After dinner, I moved into my battle headquarters which consisted of a group of weapon slits on the shoulder of a high feature immediately overlooking the causeway. From this vantage point I could see two-thirds of my position and the remaining third was in easy reach by covered routes.

David Wilson, who was my adjutant, sat with me on the turf-covered hillside. We looked across the silvery waters of the Johore Straits on to the silhouette of Singapore Island. There was a full moon and the bright starlit tropical clusters combined to give the night a fragrant beauty. David said it was hard to imagine that in a few hours we should be fighting for our lives. It was interesting to speculate on the prospects for the morrow's battle. If the Jap followed up, it would be a tricky operation, to disengage and cover the 1,100 yards of open causeway under aimed small arms fire. For this reason, every man in the unit was equipped with a smoke generator and if the order was given, 'Withdraw Smoke', every generator was to be ignited and left in each individual's position. One thing about this battle was that the chaps on the island would have a grandstand view of our performance, so I was determined we should give them their money's worth.

David and I discussed the morale of the men in the same way that one might discuss the form of a regimental side before an important Army-Cup Match. We mentioned many officers and men who had gone down in North Malaya and wished we had them with us now. A few of the old sweats were left, particularly in the transport and armoured car platoon, but we also had a number of greensticks, out of extra-regimental employment, who were so far untested.

I had known David since the day I first joined the regiment, when he was a schoolboy walking round barracks with a catapult. His father had been my commanding officer for four years and I had learnt much of my soldiering under his ruthless tutelage. His maxim had been, '*In war you make mistakes and bullets kill. In peace-time there are no bullets but words can hurt instead*'. Now I was David's commanding officer, and in the last two days had taught him a few things he didn't know. David had endless vitality, an indefatigable sense of humour and a dauntless spirit. In the withdrawal to Johore he blew a bridge, which had been prepared for demolition and abandoned, by the resourceful combination of a hand grenade and a machine gun. The grenade he put on a girder, above the charge, and tied the fly off lever lightly down with cotton. He then got into an armoured car, drove it right up to the bridge and laid the gun on the girder. On opening fire the grenade was rolled off into the charge, the cotton snapped, the grenade exploded, off went the charge and up went the bridge.

David was our amateur explosive expert and his other accomplishments included the ability to drive railway engines, play the bagpipes and operate the cinema.

Vehicles of the main body had already been filtering across the causeway since late afternoon. I could not understand why the Japs had not dive-bombed the bridge-head all day. Apart from high-level attacks, they had left us completely alone. With a full moon, they ought to be able to hot us up all night from the air but, as usual, they took no night air action whatsoever. The odd bomber was over Singapore, and searchlights and ack-ack were occasionally in action. As night progressed, more and more vehicles rumbled slowly over the causeway. The moon was so bright that lights were unnecessary.

Our two pipers had tuned up and were playing to the men. It is traditional for Highlanders to listen to the pipes before battle. At about

11 p.m. I went round the perimeter. The men were in good fettle, there had been no incident, except that a suspicious Asiatic had approached one post and, when challenged, had run away. He was fired at by the sentry and killed. Whether or not he was a fifth columnist it is impossible to say, but he had no right to be where he was.

It is worth discussing this fifth column question for a few moments, as I have not yet referred to it in much detail. In the first place, Jap stalker snipers almost invariably made contact either in local disguise or else dressed as our troops. Furthermore, they shouted out in both English and Urdu on every possible occasion. These were forms of tactical surprise that caught us unprepared. As regards fifth column proper there is little doubt that there was a fine organisation of this nature. It was particularly intense in Kedah State, where the feeling had always been anti-British. A common form of betrayal was arrows made from banana leaves, cut crops or washing, indicating gun positions, headquarters and so forth. Locals would also act as guides and indicate our positions but, from my own experience behind the Jap lines, I have no doubt that they would do the same for us. There were stories in Singapore that local Asiatics, wearing brown high neck jumpers, were systematically passing over to the Jap lines with information. Transmitters and observation posts were reputed to be established behind our lines and I also heard stories of officers being sniped at from houses within the city. Generally speaking, though, I am opposed to placing undue credence on anything but first-hand evidence. More than once in the campaign I was greeted with remarks such as, 'Hullo, old boy, I heard you were killed last night', whereas, in point of fact, I probably hadn't even been shot at.

Early in the morning we stood-to and the men had hot sweet tea and stew. It is vitally important to start any of this sort of business on a full stomach. The main body had passed through by about 0400 hours. This was considerably earlier than anyone ever dared hope and made possible only by the Jap failure to use his air arm against the bridge-head. The outer bridge-head troops were, in consequence, now brought back and they passed through our position in the hours before the dawn. I sent our pipers down to the causeway to play through the Australian battalions of the right and centre columns and the Gordon Highlanders, who formed the left rear-guard, and at 0640 I received a message to say that I could withdraw at seven o'clock.

At 0700 hours, to the second, I gave the code signal to the assembled dispatch riders, orderlies and signallers and, one minute later, the troops emerged from their positions. It was a well-executed movement and, from my vantage point, I might have been watching a turn at the Aldershot Tattoo. Every bit of movement was covered by fire from some concealed position. Armoured cars glided from one position to another, halted and traversed their turrets. Two flights of Hurricanes tore over our heads. The sight was quite unprecedented. This was a cake walk. All we wanted were the Japs but, alas, no Japs came. It was a disappointing anti-climax, after having keyed ourselves up to concert pitch.

Down at the lock-gates the pipers had struck up and the troops swung across the causeway, still in open tactical formation, but to the accompaniment of 'Blue Bonnets over the Border'. I reported my last man over to Colonel Stewart, who was standing on the mainland by the lock-gate demolition. He was determined to be the last man on the peninsula. Funnily enough he had been the first member of the B.E.F. to land in France in 1914, so this completed a fairly unique double.

I filed on in the rear of the battalion with my adjutant, R.S.M. and orderlies. When about half a mile clear of the causeway an enormous detonation put many a stout-hearted man on his stomach. This was, however, merely the blowing of the causeway demolition. The debris went several hundred feet into the air and the spectacle was most impressive. The navy had prepared the demolition, and depth charges had been used. Being a causeway and not a bridge, it was no easy matter to destroy this communication, but a gap of over two hundred feet was breached. In addition to this hole, there were other minor obstacles such as that caused by the destruction of the lock-gates.

I now went on, riding pillion on the back of a motorcycle, to meet our transport and give the necessary embussing orders. In due course the transport arrived and turned round. The troops embussed and by about ten o'clock we were safely back in Tyersall having breakfast. The siege of Singapore had begun.

CHAPTER 10

The Calm Before the Storm

The day we arrived back in Singapore, the first and only list of gallantry awards for the campaign was announced in the papers. The Argylls had a high percentage out of the total, but a large number of the recommendations had not gone through and the priority list had been altered by some busybody on the staff. Ian Stewart had been awarded a well-deserved D.S.O. and, after lunch, we went down to the town to buy a paper and send telegrams to our families. Ian Stewart and I discussed the prospects of a siege, in as optimistic terms as we could, and decided to play golf the following day as it was Sunday. During this round, we were within whistling sound of a diarrhoea attack, but outside the range of blast and splinter effect. After this, I had a short putt for a bogey which I missed, and Ian said my nerves were in a rotten state!

In the course of the weekend the battalion received reinforcements in the shape of two companies of Royal Marines who were survivors of *Prince of Wales* and *Repulse*. Amongst these I met nearly all my old friends of Roseforce, including Davis. We got on extremely well with the marines, both in the officers' and sergeants' messes and in the barrack rooms. They were a fine lot of men and, given time for training, would undoubtedly prove themselves first class jungle troops. There were no jealousies between the marines and us. A and B Companys were Argylls, C and D Royals. H.Q. Company was mixed Argylls and marines. We did. everything together in a spirit of friendly competition and, in our spare time, football matches were organised and entertainments held afterwards, in the officers' or sergeants' mess. These activities led to the fusion of our two corps being nicknamed 'Plymouth-Argyll'.

Apart from the marines, we received a number of officer reinforcements from men who had been released from the volunteers or the police. We had so many officers that the supernumeraries were formed into a Battalion Tiger patrol platoon. Tiger patrols were a speciality of Ian Stewart's. A long time before the Jap invasion we had started training officers, N.C.O.s and men to operate independently over prolonged periods, against the enemy lines of communication. The patrols were trained to be desperately aggressive. The idea of a reconnaissance patrol, as exemplified in the manuals, was not countenanced.

Every patrol, no matter how small, was essentially a fighting patrol. For jungle warfare, this is, to my mind, the correct policy for patrol work. Operations are so mobile that information collected by reconnaissance is almost certain to be out of date by the time action can be taken on it. There were three main duties of Tiger patrols. First, to harry and destroy. Secondly, to locate jungle movement and immobilize it. Thirdly, to report by fire. To do any of these tasks successfully well trained jungle men, with first class stamina and determination, were necessary.

We had got back to the island on Saturday and on Monday we continued with our interrupted training. This went on apace till the end of the week, to the accompaniment of regular air raids and intermittent shell fire. By now most of the European women and children had been evacuated, but some still remained by their own choice. Civilian evacuation was rather a touchy subject, in consequence of the recent controversy over the Penang incident. After Penang, the government announced that there would be no further compulsory evacuations. In point of fact, the normal procedure was for the Europeans and wealthier Asiatics to drive off down country in good time before the invaders arrived. In due course, these refugees would be followed by the government officials and the Local Defence Corps and this left the forward areas free for a short period of unchecked looting on the part of the poorer communities. When contact became imminent the remaining locals melted into the jungle and there they remained until the invasion had passed through.

In the case of Penang, communication to the mainland was by ferry which, like all the other essential services, had broken down. Any evacuation could therefore only be by planned organisation and, in view of the speed with which the invaders had advanced, there was precious little time for planning, and also only limited resources at hand with which to effect the evacuation. I do not wish to comment on the evacuation of Penang as, in the first place, not knowing the factors at stake, I feel unqualified to do so. All I will say is that I am truly thankful that I did not hold any post of responsibility connected with the problem and I would like to know what sort of a show certain critics would have put up had they been in this unenviable position.

On Saturday I was detailed to go to an Umpires' Conference at General Gordon Bennett's headquarters. An exercise for our brigade, which was now back in its role of mobile reserve under Malaya Command, was scheduled for Monday. In this exercise, we were to move up and counter-attack a supposed landing in the western sector, which was held by the Australians in the north and a newly arrived Indian Brigade in the south. The conference was a complete waste of time and, after hours of sheer waffle, no one left any wiser than when he arrived. In the evening, I went and saw Archie Paris, my brigadier, and told him that the whole exercise was obviously going to be a farce and would entail nothing more than our brigade getting into buses, moving up to the Australian sector, debussing and deploying. Brigadier Paris said that if they thought he did not know how to move his brigade by motor transport they had better think again, as he had no intention of wasting his valuable time in such elementary manoeuvres.

I often used to go and have a chat with Archie Paris of an evening. Angus Macdonald, his brigade major, was my closest friend and so I was frequently in the brigade mess. I used to enjoy talking to the brigadier. He had a deep knowledge of human nature and was an experienced fighting soldier. We would discuss subjects such as morale and training. Our Jocks were very fond of Archie Paris. He could talk to them in a very natural and straightforward manner on such widely differing subjects as prostitution and drink to Administration in the Field. His unruffled manner, under fire, had also obviously won their admiration.

The only good thing that came out of the conference at A.I.F. headquarters was that I had met Victor Clarke, by accident. He was disguised in khaki and very proud of his newly acquired Gurkha hat. We arranged a luncheon date at the Tanglin Club for the following day. In spite of Archie Paris's pronouncement that he would not play in this exercise, I had to attend a further conference on Sunday. We were kept waiting a full hour after the appointed time and then the Japs delivered a couple of high-level attacks on A.I.F. headquarters, which was followed by some shelling. It was quite hot work and there were a number of casualties. After these activities, had subsided we were given some instructions by the G.S.O.2., and told to make our reconnaissances.

I went off on my motorcycle, and climbed to the top of a hill on the south-west perimeter of the island. From this vantage point I had an uninterrupted view of almost the whole island. Away to the north I could distinctly pick up Johore Bahru and the large government buildings. A Jap observation balloon was standing up, over the distant horizon, like a sausage on a stick. To the right the large oil fires indicated the naval base. To the left were the undulating hills of the western part of the island which dipped down to Tuas village on the coast.

Behind me was the sea and the wreck of a big ship in the channel, and behind my right shoulder the Kranji River rolled sluggishly to the coast. Superimposed on this magnificent panorama a battle was being enacted before my eyes. Dive-bombers were circling around in two or three places, banking over steeply and sweeping down on their targets. The bursts, from artillery concentrations, were sprouting like groups of mushrooms on hill and dale. The yatter of machine-gun fire echoed through the valleys and the roar of our own 25-pounders completed the symphony.

I decided that it there was going to be an exercise tomorrow the Japs would undoubtedly oblige by acting as enemy and, in this case, the services of umpires would be redundant. I decided to go no further with my reconnaissance and, instead, lay on my back and watched the thin wisps of fleecy cloud racing across the face of a majestic tropical sun. It was Sunday, and I thought of church and people's prayers. What right had we to pray for those we loved and for the things we wanted when thousands of innocent people were falling victim to this cruel war; not only here, in Singapore, but all over the world—China, Russia, Libya. It wasn't so much the soldiers that I thought of as all the defenceless women and children. Yes, even little German children. How could one associate all this with the Christian doctrine? The Christian doctrine, or rather its interpretation by the Church of England, seemed to me a trifle narrow against this colossal background of death and suffering. What an awful thing war really was! John Scott of Amwell had expressed it well in these lines from his poem, 'The Drum':

> To me it talks of ravaged plains,
> And burning towns, and ruined swains,
> And mangled limbs, and dying groans,
> And widows' tears, and orphans' moans;
> And all that Misery's hand bestows,

Ian Stewart in the mud at Kranji Creek

To fill the catalogue of human woes.

Yes, that was war, but there was another aspect that had something grand about it; something that brought out the finer qualities in man and prevented him from growing degenerate, soft and selfish. I think Julian Grenfell had expressed these sentiments so well in his poem 'Into Battle' that I have quoted these verses at the beginning of the book. Perhaps it was battle that was fine and war that was tragic.

I lay soliloquising for quite a time, until I realised that it was getting late and I should miss my date with Victor. We had lunch at the Tanglin Club where the menu provided a welcome change from army rations. Victor had suffered a very near miss from a bomb, during the course of the morning. He was stone deaf in one ear and definitely hard of hearing in the other. Also, the starboard side of his shirt was written off and a certain amount of grass was growing out of it, which had been firmly implanted by blast. Under these conditions conversation was a bit tricky, but Victor was completely unperturbed and we had quite a jolly little party, together with one or two friends whom we picked up at the bar. These included Ford, the gunner, with whom I had driven to Kuala Selangor, and Warren of the marines. Ford told me that Patrick Don had been badly wounded in Johore and they feared he would lose his legs. I believe he was evacuated and, eventually, recovered completely. I sincerely hope so as he was a first-rate fighting soldier and a good chap to have around in a battle.

During the afternoon, the enemy artillery and mortar preparations continued to hot up. By nightfall there was a continuous rumble of gunfire and musketry from the whole northern half of the perimeter. It was obvious that the Japs were going to attack that night. Apart from the barrage, the conditions of moon and tide conformed to those under which the Japs invariably undertook amphibious operations. That is to say, there was a waning moon which didn't rise till 2 a.m. and also a flow tide at the same time. The first flights would beach under cover of complete darkness and then have the moon to assist them in exploiting inshore. These were the conditions at Kota Bahru and these were the conditions in almost every single operation which the Japs had carried out in China. They were probably the best trained and equipped troops in the world at this particular form of warfare.

We sat in the ante-room after dinner listening to the battle. The colonel looked grave. I knew his thoughts were the same as mine. I knew neither of us had confidence in the beach defences. I had seen quite a bit of the western perimeter in the last week. The troops were very thin on the ground. Posts were not mutually supporting; there was very little depth; there were inadequate reserves; the field works were flimsy as digging was impracticable on account of the high-water level. The earth stockades that I had seen wouldn't stand up to the barrage which I was now hearing.

The colonel stated his opinion that the Japs would land on the north-cast of the island. There had already been contact in that sector on Pulau Ubin, an island lying in the Straits of Johore. I ventured that the landing would be in the north-west and backed my argument by the facts of the bombing and artillery concentrations that the Japs had put down in the Aussies' sector that morning. The colonel was interested to hear about this and we discussed the pros and cons. I suggested that a determining factor would be the psychological one, of which troops in the island the Japs considered most susceptible to punishment. These remarks initiated quite a heated discussion, and Ian settled the matter by wisely suggesting that we should go to bed and get all the rest we could, while the going was good.

I went down to my hut and laid out my best pair of ironed and starched drill shorts and shirt for the morrow. I then checked over all my equipment, put fresh water in my water bottle, filled my pack and climbed into bed. Almost before my head touched the pillow I was asleep. The next thing I knew was that David Wilson was standing over me with a torch. I looked at my watch. It was 4 a.m.

'I suppose', I said, 'the little bleeders have landed.'

'Yes', David replied, 'they're ashore in the Aussie sector. We're at one hour's notice to move from 0600 hours. There are no further orders. I take it everything's Oke in your company. I'll get along now and tell the others.'

CHAPTER 11

The Battle of Singapore

I was in command of Headquarter Company which was a rotten job for a battle as my sub-units, which consisted of the armoured cars, mortars and Tiger patrol platoon, all came directly under the tactical control of the commanding officer. Of course, if the C.O. became a casualty then I would take over but, until then, I was merely in command of rear or administrative headquarters, which consisted of the medical platoon (who were Chinese Volunteers), and the transport.

After completing an immaculate toilet, I went down to my company lines. Everything was in order and the vehicles had been loaded the previous day in anticipation of a move. In the fighting part of the transport, apart from weapons and ammunition, we carried a reserve of two days' hard rations and three days' tea, milk and sugar. This was split up amongst all the vehicles so that it would be possible to fight, cut off, for quite a time.

After breakfast, there was nothing to do but wait. The sun came up and, shortly afterwards, enemy aircraft became active. We sat lounging about in the mess drinking tea and speculating as to how the battle was progressing. The roar of aircraft engines was superimposed on the distant rumble of gun and rifle fire and occasionally the local air sentry would sound the alarm which meant that aircraft were heading in our direction and that it was time to get within whistling distance of a slit trench. We all had our own slit trenches in the little garden outside the mess hut—the height of comfort. These were carefully allotted so that a direct hit on a trench would not knock out two key men; for instance, the colonel and I were in different trenches.

There was rather a good programme of music on the wireless and, at about ten o'clock, this was interrupted and an announcement made to the effect that the Japs had landed in some strength on the north-west of the island and that we were dealing with the situation. This was somewhat of a mystery. If the Japs were in 'some strength', the local reserve, which amounted only to a battalion, would be unable to deal with the situation and here we were, the only command reserve, still awaiting orders.

Eventually a dispatch rider arrived waving a message. David Wilson bounded forward to receive it and other officers crowded round in eager expectancy. The message read, 'Your allotment of the grenade range of the following dates is cancelled'. This absurdity relieved the tension and induced an element of humour into what was really rather a tense atmosphere. It was very like waiting in the pavilion with one's pads on and the score board reading 25 runs for 5 wickets. Yes, we were next to bat all right and it looked very much as if the shine was still on the ball. We laughed at this fairly apt analogy and wondered what objective we would be given for a counter-attack. The minutes ticked slowly by. Would this waiting never end? I had drunk enough tea to float a battleship—then the telephone rang.

'This is the Brigade Major speaking.'

'Hello Angus, Angus speaking,' I replied. 'Any orders;'

'Yes, how soon can you move;'

'We can be on parade in five minutes.'

'All right, get the men on parade. Orders will be round in ten minutes.' Our orders were to move up in transport to a rendezvous at the 'Neck'. This was a place on the Tengah road between the source of the Kranji and Jurong Rivers. The transport was already formed up, in a concealed harbour area, outside the camp. The troop-carrying vehicles moved up and we embussed on the 'platform' system. The guide group was sent on ahead to the 'Neck', to put us into harbour on arrival at the far end. Our orders were to move at 20 miles in the hour and 15 vehicles to the mile and not to stop for enemy air attacks or shelling. This was a battle move and we were to go straight through. Our road discipline was hampered by other units using the same route.

Many of the drivers were blinding along in rather a panicky manner and often pulling to a sharp halt and disgorging a posse of troops, who would fling themselves into ditches, in anticipation of bombs. This put me in a black rage. Panic is very infectious and I did not want our men to be contaminated by this undignified behaviour. Well-disciplined troops will remain steady and calm under severe conditions because each individual receives confidence from the security that he, personally, derives from the mass. This confidence overcomes his individual fear and, in that way, he directly contributes to the steadiness of the unit as a whole. The inculcation *of esprit de corps* is the means to which this is the end.

Esprit de corps, to my mind, implies the voluntary submission of the individual to the requirements of the whole. Human nature being what it is, the voluntary state is only achieved by forceful methods in the initial stages. It is brought to fruition by personal example, by tradition, by public opinion and honour. It entails giving all and taking nothing; but the dividend comes in all right when death is close at hand, and to have experienced the exhilaration of this spirit, when all else seems to have gone, is a privilege which I, for one, have appreciated more than any other mercy that providence has ever bestowed on me.

We arrived at the 'Neck' and our guides piloted us into dispersed harbour. As soon as the troops had debussed we started to dig slit trenches as, with the Jap 'daisy-cutting' anti-personnel bombs, ground level is 100 per cent dangerous. Hardly was the top soil off than a high-level attack developed. Down came the bombs, chiefly on rear battalion H.Q. and the two marine companies. There were quite a few casualties.

Mike Blackwood, who commanded the armoured car platoon came up and asked me if I'd go and help at an Australian Gunner Command Post where there were a number of casualties. The major's arm had been blown off. Two or three men were dead and there were several wounded. Luckily there was a doctor and ambulance to hand and the wounded were soon evacuated. The Australians asked me what they should do with the dead and I suggested that they should bury them where they were. This was their first blooding and I could see they were appalled by the sight of the dead men with their glassy eye-balls turned upwards and their swollen tongues lolling idly in their gaping mouths. I straightened the bodies out so that they could be easily buried after *rigor mortis* had set in and collected their red identity discs and valuables and handed them over, tied up in a handkerchief, to the senior Digger. After this we walked back to H.Q.

Michael said: 'I don't know how you can do all that stuff and not care a damn. I feel it all most terribly. I'd give anything not to.'

'It's no good letting it worry you, Mike,' I said. 'You have just got to treat dead men like bacon and you must steel yourself to look at wounds, and do what you can to help. I wish to hell I knew more about first aid. If ever I get out of this, I'm going to learn it up. It's awful feeling you might be doing the wrong thing. Thank God there was a medico on the spot.'

'If ever I get out of this,' replied Michael, 'I shall never take anything for granted again. One didn't realise how damned lucky one was, and half the good things in life one never appreciated.'

Michael was a very sensitive officer, but that did not prevent him from putting himself in places of danger which duty necessitated. He was a veritable Jonah, as far as bombs were concerned, and wherever Michael went the Japanese bombers were sure to follow; on the same principle as Mary and her little lamb. He had a very narrow escape the following afternoon in Bukit Timah village, when a Jap bomb registered a direct hit on one of our armoured cars, and a splinter grazed a broad welt across his forehead.

By this time another high-level attack was shaping in our direction. We went over to a slit trench which had been dug previously and dropped in. There were a couple of Jocks in occupation already and, as they were looking a bit dejected, I offered them cigarettes. The aircraft were now directly overhead and the whistling started, so down we got and another of those deafening series of explosions took place. When it was over I wondered, what had become of my C.S.M. whom I hadn't seen since we arrived.

'Bing,' I called out.

'Yessir,' came the answer.

'Where the hell are you;'

'Sitting in the car, Sir.'

'Well get out and come into this trench.'

'Very good, Sir.'

C.S.M. Bing cared less than nothing about bombing. He was a fatalist and quite fearless. In Northern Malaya, he had distinguished himself, together with Bal Hendry, his company commander, when the two of them accounted for some sixteen odd Japs single-handed. Bal had a detachment watching a railway line and, during the course of the day, he went there together with Bing and his runner. Whilst inspecting the post, they saw a party of Japs come down the railway line and disappear into the station. Bal decided on an immediate encircling attack in which the detachment should act as the holding force and he, Bing and the runner the striking force. On arrival at the station Bal attacked the ticket office and ordered Bing to protect his flank and rear.

The plan worked admirably. Bal had a fight on his own in the ticket office, killing four or five Japs as a preliminary to capturing the remaining two. Bing, stalking round the outside of the building, was presented with the sight of ten Japanese backsides working their way forward to help in the ticket office fight. He tore off a whole Tommy gun slide at this target, killing the lot, and then rushed in to help Bal who was engaged in a vicious hand-to-hand struggle on the floor. Bing, seizing his Tommy gun by the red hot barrel, dispatched one Jap with ease and Bal cracked the other one with his tin hat sufficiently gently to enable them to remove a live prisoner. With this prize, they executed an orderly withdrawal and returned safely to battalion headquarters. A few days later Bal was severely wounded and subsequently evacuated to India and Bing was also one of the few who survived this disastrous campaign. Fortune favours the brave—yes, sometimes. On the other hand, neither of them was decorated for this gallant and skilfully conducted fight.

After the second high level-attack we were treated to a series of dive-bombing ordeals and then a message came from the C.O. to say that we were to leave the transport and move forward to a specified assembly position. A rendezvous was given for the 'Orders Group' and we were instructed not to halt and take cover for dive-bombing or artillery fire. At 'Orders' we were told that the position was serious. The Australians had been driven well back and there was a chance that the Japs might succeed in breaking through down the Tengah Road. We were, therefore, to occupy a position astride this road. Localities were pointed out on the map and on the ground and the companies went forward in occupation of these dispositions. It was disappointing that we were not put in to attack, as most of us knew this part of the island very well and a successful counter-attack would have been good for morale. Without having been forward to see the situation at the time, it is impossible to say if this was the correct tactical solution or not. We were under command of Gordon Bennett and these were his orders.

Dive-bombing and cannon attacks were pretty vicious. To give an idea of the intensity, we took four dive-bomber attacks, by formations of nine aircraft in each assault, at one particular spot inside ten minutes. I had an uncomfortable drive back down the road, to give orders to our troop-carrying and 'A' echelon transport, and I had my vehicle riddled with cannon shells and the radiator punctured, in consequence of which she seized up. This didn't matter much, as the vehicle in question had already been abandoned in the middle of the road and didn't belong to us.

Rear headquarters, of which I was in charge, was sited some 500 yards behind the forward companies. We were a pathetic little gathering consisting of Bing, my driver, my two orderlies and myself. Later on, we received an armoured car and with this force, whose fire power amounted to one Tommy gun, two rifles, my revolver, and the armoured car's machine gun, we formed a little locality on the road. The doctor and the *padre* I had sent further to the rear where better facilities existed for treating the wounded. On a small feature to our right, a 3.7-inch ack-ack battery was located.

After we had been in position some time small detachments of Australian troops started to filter in. These were survivors from the forward defended localities and, as the day wore on, more and more Aussies passed through us. They had obviously been through a stiff ordeal and they bore marks of the battle, being either caked in mud from the mangrove swamps or soaked by the rivers they had swum in their cross-country withdrawal. All were enshrouded in the fog of war, having lost touch with their neighbouring units and headquarters. I collected the designations and numbers of each sub-unit that passed through us which provided a useful source of information to those that followed. Most of them were surprised to find that they were not the only survivors of their own particular unit and it is a curious but undeniable fact that, in defeat, troops are always convinced that their own casualties are heavier than is really the case.

During the afternoon, we were encouraged to see some of our few remaining Hurricanes engaged in successful dog-fights with enemy aircraft. The dive-bombing eased off in the afternoon, but by now we were enshrouded in a pall of smoke from the countless petrol fires which seemed to have set the whole island alight. The Japs were in complete possession of Tengah aerodrome which was not far from our present position. Our artillery were blazing away and shells were whistling overhead continuously. During the day, I learnt to differentiate between the whistle of a shell which necessitates the prone or horizontal position being adopted and the whistle which indicates that the burst will be sufficiently far away to allow the vertical position to be retained.

With the gathering darkness, the steady afternoon drizzle turned into a downpour. The 'B' echelon vehicles arrived up and we consumed welcome tea and stew. The night passed uneventfully and before light the orders group was sent for at battalion H.Q., which was established in a humble Chinese house a few hundred yards up the road.

The position seemed a trifle obscure. The Jap landing in the north-west of the island had been completely successful and the troops in the southwest were now threatened in the rear, so the whole of this sector had to be abandoned and the plan was to reconstitute a new line behind our present position. Some Australians came into position on our left and we were to hold this as a kind of rear-guard till 0900 hours. The ack-ack battery on my right had already received orders to destroy their pieces, and those for whom rifles could be found remained to fight in their position.

It was still pitch black when I arrived at battalion headquarters and with the first streaks of light I suddenly noticed that I was standing around with a lot of African troops, but these transpired to be my brother officers. What had happened was that the rain had brought down with it volumes of carbonised oil and now we were black as pitch from head to foot. The whole countryside was in the same condition—the trees, the grass, the roads and the water in the ditches. After orders, we had some breakfast; tea and stew again, and then a shave with ditch-water. It is most important to make the men shave, no matter how bad the conditions. Sometimes the situation doesn't permit of one, but there is nearly always some moment in the day when it is possible to have a quick scratch round, providing there is sufficient water. You will seldom see a shaved unit in a bad state of morale.

No sooner was the sun up than the dive-bombers got cracking again. Dive-bombing is actually a misnomer, for the Jap does not go in for the steep Teutonic power-dive. Instead of this, he goes into a more or less shallow glide and often does not pull out till a remarkably low altitude. The speed and angle of the glide varied with different pilots. The usual form was to let off cannon on the downward glide and then release a stick of three bombs before pulling out. Sometimes there would be only one bomb. It was possible to see the bombs being released, if one was not screened by trees and, from this, to decide whether or not to lie down.

Bing and I were taking turns with the Tommy gun and enjoying a good morning's sport at the dive-bombers. I would not go so far as to say that we brought any down in flames, but the bombers gave the impression of showing considerable respect for our fire and some of them were so low that we could hardly have missed.

It was my turn with the 'John Roscoe'. Bing was filling magazines and Private Fletcher was cave-dwelling in a filthy ditch.

'Get out of that ditch, Fletcher, and fire at the aircraft,' roared Bing.

Fletcher emerged looking rather like a whipped spaniel. After a bit, there was a report from Fletcher's rifle.

'What the hell are you on, Fletcher?' shouted Bing.

'I wis jist firin' at yon aeroplane, Surr,' replied Fletcher.

'Well, that plane's too bloody far out,' retorted Bing. 'It's just a waste of ammunition.'

I couldn't help laughing at Bing's condemnation of Fletcher's solitary shot. Our own 9.2-inch were firing over our heads at Tengah aerodrome and there must have been several hundred pounds' worth of explosive in the air at any given minute. Just then a nice bird came over to my left, which I engaged with three bursts.

'There you are, Fletcher,' said Bing. 'See how the major does it. You've got to wait for it, me lad. See, Fletcher, wait for it. Now carry on in your own time.' Then as an afterthought: 'Not bad at all, Sir. In fact, just about a bull's-eye.' Bing professed to be able to see the line of fire, so this was encouraging. Unfortunately, we had no tracer. It would have been nice to have had a Bren gun and plenty of tracer, and I think we might have got some kills. Fletcher told me, later in the day, that he was very glad that he had been dug out and told to shoot at the dive-bombers, as it made him feel as brave as a lion.

By about 7.45 a.m. odd bullets started to whip overhead and it was a bit of a mystery where these came from. Soon afterwards our forward companies were in contact. There was quite heavy firing from the front and we came under fire from Jap 2-inch mortars. One of these bombs (or it may have been a grenade from a discharge cup) burst within a few feet of me and did no damage whatever.

Ian Stewart came back shortly after 8 a.m. and said he was sending back A Company and that I was to organise a 'lay-back' to cover out the rest of the forward troops. The ack-ack battery was to come under my command and I was to delay as long as possible, subject to not becoming pinned down. These are most unsatisfactory orders to receive because, if you get out intact, you have probably left too early, whereas the first indication of serious contact may well be firing to your rear and, in this case, you will probably be pinned.

I made a reconnaissance of the area and gave the necessary instructions to the ack-ack gunners. We fixed up a visual signal, from respective viewpoints in our two areas, for initiating the withdrawal. A Company, commanded by my cousin Michael Bardwell, started to trickle back. There were remarkably few of them and, apart from Sgt. Wallace, hardly one experienced N.C.O. amongst the lot. I got a weak perimeter formed which more or less linked up with the gunners on the right, but I could not stop infiltration to the right of the road, and my left flank was in the air.

A few walking wounded started trickling past. David Wilson, who had accompanied Ian Stewart on his visit, had got a rifle bullet through the barrel of his Tommy-gun and this he pointed out to me with great glee. Aylwin, Captain of Marines, came through, with blood pouring from a bullet wound in the forearm, which he was staunching with an improvised bandage made from his map. At 0900 hours, the forward troops withdrew and shortly after this we came under aimed but inaccurate small arms fire from the ridge in front. It was almost impossible to recognise a target on account of a ground haze which, superimposed on the heavy mantle of carbonised oil, made lines and shapes indistinguishable.

Occasionally one got glimpses of movement between the trees, but nothing one could guarantee to hit. The Japs, though, were in an even worse position, as regards visibility, as we were fighting with the sun at our backs. They had got fire to bear on the armoured car which was on the road a few yards to my right. Bullets were whanging against the plating and ricocheting off. I got hit on the knee by some 'splash' from the armoured car but, apart from tuning me up a trifle, it did no damage, although the puncture took three months to heal.

Some of the men started moving back and we had to take a firm line over this before it developed into a rot. The lack of experienced officers, N.C.O.s and old soldiers was very noticeable. I had got Sgt. Wallace and a couple of marines watching the gap between us and the ack-ack battery, but they could not cover the whole of this area and when firing started from this direction there was some cause for anxiety, and I had to decide whether or not this constituted a threat to my communications. In view of the fact that it was not vital for us to hold this 'lay-back' position and that my orders were not to be pinned I reluctantly decided to order the withdrawal, but I was still in two minds as to whether I was not being a trifle gutless. The point about this 'lay-back' position was that it was very hastily organised and, with insufficient troops, it did not constitute a sound tactical locality.

On the left of the road, and to the rear of our position, there was a large expanse of jungle clearance, and it would be necessary for us to withdraw to the back of the young orchard, in which we were now disposed, and then cross the road, so as to take advantage of the abundant cover on the far side. The Japs were firing light automatics down the road and I expected we would have quite a few casualties crossing this fire lane. However, their shooting was just the bottom and, by sending men across in small groups at the double, we succeeded in getting away with it.

On the far side of the road we passed some Australian troops who had a 3-inch mortar detachment in action. I got this piece directed on to the area from which I reckoned the Jap automatic fire was coming and left them dropping eggs down the spout. After a few hundred yards, we joined up with the rest of the battalion, which was dispersed in harbour. Here we remained for an hour or so, until orders arrived telling us that we were to take up depth dispositions on the high ground west of the main road which ran from Singapore to the Johore causeway. Once out of contact we came in for another continuous dose ot dive-bombing. The only let up that we had from this form of attack was when we were in ground action.

We marched back down the road to Bukit Panjang and established battalion headquarters at the P.W.D. quarries on the main road. The two marine companies were kept in reserve and the two Argyll companies disposed on the reverse slopes of the high ground. The bombing attacks continued unceasingly till late in the afternoon and then eased off. We now received orders to withdraw our two forward companies and to take as much rest during the night as possible, prior to launching a counterattack the next day. The Japs were reported to be in possession of our side of the causeway and to have advanced as far as Mandai village, which was a few miles up the road to our right flank. 18th Division had counterattacked Mandai village and found it unoccupied. I went on a liaison visit to our forward companies, to give them instructions for the night. On crossing the railway line, I came under harassing mortar fire. These were the Jap long-range 4-inch mortars. They were an effective weapon with almost twice the range of our 3-inch mortar, and they were invariably well handled.

By nightfall we had the two marine companies and battalion headquarters established in a rough locality inside some rubber trees near the P.W.D. quarry, and the two Argyll companies about three-quarters of a mile to the right and also in the rubber. Both localities were a few hundred yards from the main road which ran parallel to our front.

Before the light failed I went for a short walk, with the colonel, up the slope which lay behind us, on to the Government Dairy Farm.

2ND ARGYLL & SUTHERLAND HIGHLAND OFFICERS AND NCOS AT A BRIEFING ON A RUBBER PLANTATION, MALAYA 1941

Here was a broad expanse of country not unlike the Sussex Downs. Ian said it made him feel a different man to get a view of something approximating to England. By this time there was a good deal of small arms fire coming from the high ground immediately to the west of the main road. This sector was being held by Indian troops and Ian and I agreed that it was almost certain that the Japs would break through during the night and that we would be committed before our intended counter-attack could be staged. Ian said that if there was a box-up during the night he would rally the battalion on the Dairy Farm where good fields of fire existed.

We returned to battalion H.Q. in the gathering darkness in time for the usual evening meal of tea and stew. I had a premonition of disaster that night and, as I had lost my identity disc in *Kudat,* when she was sunk, I wrote my name and rank in my diary and asked the finder to send it to my wife's address.

Ian gave out orders for the conduct of the defence during the night. We were to remain in position facing outwards. There was to be no firing (as this would only result in shooting upon our side) and the password was 'Argyll'.

About 11 o'clock, the brigadier and Angus Macdonald arrived. Archie Paris announced that he had been up the road and that a Jap tank had suddenly appeared and fired at him. He had returned the fire with his revolver and the tank had swung round and withdrawn but, he added, 'I expect he'll be back soon with a few pals'. He told Ian to organise some anti-tank defences astride the main road and then, turning to Angus said, 'You go off to Bukit Timah. Tell the Aussies what's happened and get a proper obstacle covered by anti-tank guns fixed up. We'll hold 'em here as long as we can', and then, as a parting shot, after Angus was already on his way, 'and after you've done that put some soda on the ice'. Old Archie was a great believer in his creature comforts. The brigade mess was always the acme of comfort, even if a battle was in progress. Archie would not countenance shoddy living and the high standard on which he insisted, during manoeuvres, undoubtedly accounted for the fact that we were such a well administered unit under war conditions.

Obstacles were hastily organised astride the road opposite our two localities. Ours consisted of four or five vehicles which we lined across the road and covered with an armoured car and an anti-tank rifle. In front of this a row of anti-tank mines was quickly armed and laid by David Wilson. Before long we heard heavy firing up the road which indicated that the Japs were in contact with the two Argyll companies. One of our armoured cars came back and reported that its armament had been knocked out by a Jap tank.

We were lying down in a circle facing outwards. Michael Blackwood and Davis of the marines were down at the road block. Some Indian troops, who had melted from their positions on the high ground west of the main road, straggled through our position. Someone let off a rifle and hit one of our officers in the stomach. The night was as black as the Earl of Hell's waistcoat and you couldn't see a thing. I sat with my back against a tree and dozed off to sleep. I was awakened by the sound of tank tracks on the tarmac. Three long bursts of fire were smacked into our position. These were point 8-inch explosive bullets. They made an ugly sound as they hit their mark and the fiery streams of tracer pierced the darkness like red hot pokers.

Our armoured car and the anti-tank rifle returned the fire and the tanks withdrew. Firing was still continuing from the high ground on the far side of the road, but there was deathly stillness in our little bit of jungle. Then the stillness was broken. I heard approaching footsteps and the clink of equipment. 'Jap infantry,' I thought. We would get trodden on and then there would be God's own shemozzle. The steps came nearer. I sensed a man coming up to me. He stopped and then I clearly heard him get down into the lying position and pull back the cocking handle of his light automatic.

My heart was pounding so heavily that I thought it would give me away. I drew my pistol and cocked the action. I comforted myself that, if this Samurai opened up, he would almost certainly fire high and, from the light of the muzzle flash, I would be able to nail him with my pistol, as the range could only be a matter of a few feet. Nothing happened and then, after a bit, the footsteps went on. It was impossible to say if they were going at right angles or parallel to the road.

Shortly after this more tanks appeared and a heavy fire-fight developed between our road block and the Jap tanks. The latter were making steady progress and their weight of fire was incomparably heavier than ours. A loud explosion and a vivid flash followed by another announced that the Japs tanks had closed with our block and that David's mines had found their mark. Then the firing ceased.

Ian Stewart came up to me. 'Is that you, Angus?' he whispered.

'Yes, sir,' I replied.

'Look, I want you to go down to the road block and see what's happening. Take someone with you.'

Men of the Argyll and Sutherland Highlanders on a patrol of jungle roads in Malaya during the Second World War – December 1941

'Right, sir. I'll take Bing. I know where he is.'

Bing and I felt our way step by step down the track to the road When we arrived there was no sign at all of our road block. The vehicles had vanished and a long stream of Jap tanks was milling slowly past. They were much more silent than our tracked vehicles and, at this speed, they hardly made a sound. It was so dark that, even standing on the road, it was only just possible to see the vehicles in dim outline. Even if we had had a few Molotov cocktails (which were the only type of anti-tank grenade in Malaya) we could not have done much good; as the road was very broad and there was a wide grass verge on the far side, so that knocking out a couple of tanks would not have stemmed the advance. We just stood there watching this procession for quite a few minutes, feeling entirely impotent with the weapons at our disposal.

We returned to battalion H.Q. and I reported to the C.O. Things looked bad. The Japs might quite possibly break through into Singapore that night. In point of fact, they were successfully stopped at Bukit Timah village by Angus Macdonald's road block. Angus actually drove the last vehicle into the block under the fire of the leading Jap tank. Archie Paris and Angus, between them, undoubtedly saved Singapore that night, as prior to Archie's initial encounter no one knew that the Jap had brought tanks across from the mainland. Once they had captured the causeway it was comparatively easy for them to bridge the demolition as they had had all the previous week for bringing forward the requisite stores. However, I believe these tanks actually crossed in landing craft and did not come over the causeway.

Once back at battalion H.Q. I returned to my own position. I had no idea of the time as my watch was not luminous, but judged it to be about 3 or 4 a.m. Someone about a hundred yards away was talking very loud in Urdu. I decided to go and stop this and walked off towards the sound of the voices. On my way, I heard other voices talking. I listened. It sounded something like Urdu but I couldn't recognise any words. Then someone put on a torch and I saw a whole platoon of Japanese infantry standing beside a lorry. They were wearing helmets, packs and full equipment. They were all dressed the same and not in the informal attire of the cyclists whom I had seen on the Temerloh raid. I suspected they were a unit of the Imperial Guard.

The torch went out and then someone started to shout out in the inimitable accents of a well-educated Indian, 'Are there any Indian troops here?'

Lanchester 6x4 armoured car in Malaya

The shouting continued. 'The war's over. There's no more fighting. All British troops come this way.' Anyone from B or C Companies over here, please.'

I removed my tin hat, and stood flattened against a tree. A Jap bumped into me and murmured what I took to be an apology. The shouting continued.

'Are there any British troops here?'

I heard one of our new officers in the Tiger patrol platoon call out, 'Yes'.

'You bloody fool,' I thought to myself. 'Now you've bought it.' That officer never turned up again.

I thought this was no place for Rose, so I retraced my steps towards battalion H.Q. When I got there, I could find nobody. I went to the abandoned bivouac tent where I knew Weir, the wounded officer, was lying. He was not there so I rightly deduced that Ian had taken the troops out to the flank, to the prearranged rendezvous on the dairy farm. As I had a couple of primed grenades in my haversack, I fancied it might be considered supportable to portion out one of these amongst the guardsmen on the track. Since our chaps had now withdrawn, the restriction on night firing would be automatically lifted and there was negligible risk to myself in throwing a missile.

The jungle is a sanctuary for small parties, even by day, so, alone in the jungle on a dark night, I would acquire a degree of security analogous to that of a maiden's virginity in a convent. I therefore set off cat-walking in the direction of the track but, after covering some distance, I continued to find myself alone and unorientated. Consequently I pulled out my compass and was surprised to find the needle pointing in a completely different direction to what I expected. For all I knew I had completed a grand circle or a figure of eight. Anyhow, I knew the dairy farm was due east of our original location, so I set my compass at 90 degrees for night marching and sneaked ahead with an uncomfortable feeling that the compass was telling a lie.

After some progress, I heard movement on my right, so I froze against a tree; pistol in right hand and compass in left. Some bodies were bearing down on me, without any mistake, and I was relieved to hear some timber crack, to the accompaniment of that common and illogically applied Anglo-Saxon word that serves for such a high percentage of the British soldier's vocabulary. The *chasseurs* turned out to be three of our marines. They were going unconcernedly in a northerly direction, through no fault of their own as they hadn't a compass, so I took them in tow with me and, before long, we struck a track which I was confident would lead us to the dairy farm. We were soon clear of the jungle and, shortly afterwards, one of our own sentry groups brought us to a halt. Here I met the colonel who was in some anxiety about my absence, as a rumour had already been circulated reporting me as killed.

Ian told me that the brigadier had taken a party back across country to Sime road, and that he was going to dispose the Tiger patrol platoon on the Dairy Farm, with orders to harass and delay the enemy on that line of approach, till dark the same night. Before long the first streaks of dawn appeared to our rear and the Tiger patrol positions were completed. There was heavy artillery fire to our right rear and this was probably 18th Division's counter-attack. To our left flank there was the sound of battle in the vicinity of Bukit Timah village.

Our party consisted of Ian, David Wilson, Bing, Corporal Masterton, a few Jocks and myself. We went back to Sime road on a compass bearing through the jungle. It was quite a long plug and there was some fairly thick undergrowth to combat. On the way, we passed a small party of Indian stragglers and I relieved one of these of his Tommy gun as he showed no indication of having any intention of putting it to any good use.

We came out on the familiar features of the golf course and walked across to the club house where some Bofors gunners gave us a cup of tea and a 'wad'. Ian then went to report at Command Headquarters and the rest of us lay in a bunker and watched the Bofors and other light ack-ack blazing away at the Jap planes, which were roaring over low enough to knock your hat off. The shooting was extremely wild and inaccurate and we very often had to flatten ourselves to avoid being hit by our own ack-ack.

Our orders were to go back into reserve and re-organise as much as we could, prior to being sent up the line again. Our 'B' echelon transport and our reserves of ammunition and equipment were already awaiting us in a hutted camp and thither we went. When I arrived at this place I found it stuffed full of cave-dwellers. These included a representative of the Command Paymaster's Branch and I took the opportunity of bringing him to the surface and cashing a Field Service cheque for the maximum sum admissible. This amounted to about £10. I gave all this money to my Chinese boy, Ah Ling, who was faithfully awaiting my return, and bade him take his leave, which he did with tearful eyes and religious blessings. There was no arrogance on the part of the Chinese that I ever encountered in this our hour of humiliation.

Archie Paris's small party of mixed Argylls and marines was already in the camp but there was no sign of anyone from either of the two Argyll companies. In fact, they had not been heard of since the Jap tank attack had developed against them on the previous night, in spite of the several efforts that we had made to contact them by means of orderlies and patrols.

I heard many months later, from Sergeant Wallace, who was one of the few survivors, that they had remained in their position till dawn when they found themselves isolated and surrounded by Japs on all sides. They had then split into small parties and done their best to break through to a rallying point on the pipe line which connected Singapore to the Johore causeway. This pipe line went straight through the jungle and was a well-known landmark to all of us in the regiment. Most of the parties, I fear, never got through but I came across the following account of operations in a newspaper, sometime subsequently, and I think it is worth quoting as a tribute to the many Jocks that muse have fallen unseen and unapplauded:

> The Argyll and Sutherland Highlanders—the regiment which formed the famous Thin Red Line at Balaclava in 1854—have added new glory to their history by an exploit at Singapore, made known last night. A detachment of the regiment, after covering the retreat of British and Indian troops was cut off from support with no hope of escape. Its last job was to hold the pipe line. Three of the men, ragged, exhausted, burned deep red by the sun, carrying rifles and a Bren gun and bayonets stained with Japanese blood, gave the "thumbs-up" signal as they made their way through a British Force holding another position. An officer advised them to get some sleep instead of making for the pipe line, which could be approached only by crossing positions held by the Japanese. "My orders were to join the battalion there, sir," replied the corporal in charge. "If we're the last of the battalion I'm the senior N.C.O. My last order was to hold the pipe line. If the C.O.'s alive he'll be expecting us. If he isn't he'll expect us to be at the pipe line. So, we'll be moving off, sir."

Sergeant Wallace's party had two encounters with the Japs. In one of these they were surprised at short range and the officer in command of the party, Captain Napier, was killed in the act of charging with his drawn revolver. Another officer, called Love, was leapt on by a Jap, who half-throttled him with his own pistol lanyard, but a Jock shot the assailant in the seat of the pants and Love escaped, while the Samurai was left bellowing on the ground.

After seeing to my men, I took a shower bath and a change of clothes to the accompaniment of an artillery duel between one of our own batteries, which was just outside the camp, and some Jap guns at an unknown place. The Jap shells were whistling just over the tops of the huts and occasionally a short one would hit a tree or the roof of a building. There was one continuous series of air raids throughout the day and both high-level and dive bombing attacks were intermixed without interruption.

Refreshed from my toilet I made a tour of the camp and had the good fortune to meet another Field Cashier out of whom I managed to wheedle a further eighty dollars. We spent the latter half of the morning implementing an order to break up all the liquor in the camp. This particular denial scheme was systematically and effectively carried out throughout the island and, however distasteful the work proved to be, it was certainly a sound measure in view of the Jap's weakness for strong spirits.

After luncheon, at which I enjoyed a little *Chablis* freshly off the ice, I was sent for to take orders from the brigadier, in place of Ian Stewart, who was resting.

At orders the brigadier informed us that there was a hole in the Australian line, which had been reformed two or three miles to the east of Bukit Timah village. The remnants of our brigade were to fill this hole and our dispositions and boundaries were indicated on the map. We were to be in occupation by 1700 hours. The orders were perfectly clear. There was plenty of time and I knew the particular area like the back of my hand, so this was easy money as I could dispense with all reconnaissance, apart from contacting the units on my flanks.

I returned to the orderly room and was in the process of writing a warning order for the move when a roar of dive-bombers and the crash of exploding bombs cause the composition walls to flex in and out like a sheet of clastic. A splinter cut clean through the desk and, whilst on the point of continuing with my interrupted message writing, I noticed a horde of Indians running past the open doorway. I went out on to the veranda to see what the flap was about and noticed that a brisk fire had started to leeward.

The ubiquitous Bing was already on the spot dealing with casualties and organising stretcher-bearer parties. I rang up for the Fire Services but the line was cut and, furthermore, I discovered subsequently that the water main was also cut and belching its contents freely over the road. Our own firefighting equipment was as much use as a wheelbarrow in a sailing boat, so the conflagration raged unchecked, assisted by a dry, fresh wind, almost unknown in Malaya.

Archie Paris, hatless and smoking a cheroot, now appeared on the scene, with Angus Macdonald.

'I'm delighted,' said Angus, 'to see that ruddy officers' latrine burnt down and I must say it's going up in fine style.'

Archie suggested that I got a party organised to move the ammunition. 'Particularly the mortar ammunition,' he added, 'we want all we've got of that.'

I had already got men working on moving the vehicles and armoured cars to safety, and we soon had a chain of men passing ammunition boxes from the guard room. The Jocks were getting down to the stevedore work with such a will that orders were redundant.

By the time, we had completed this task the fire which had originated by the orderly room had burnt out all the men's lines and now another fire, echeloned to the rear of the first one, was burning through the officers' quarters and mess. We were bent on saving all the fighting equipment on which we could lay our hands and this we did to the intermittent accompaniment of the Japanese dive-bombers which came over periodically and plastered the camp with machine-gun and cannon fire.

Whilst all this was going on a private soldier came up to me with a broad grin on his face and a grenade in his hand. 'Shall I throw this in the fire, sir?' he said.

I saw he had gone clean nuts. 'No,' I replied, 'I wouldn't do that.' 'Well, it might help to put it out.'

'Yes,' I said smilingly, 'but we don't want to put it out just yet. You give me the grenade and I'll let you do it later.'

He had already withdrawn and thrown away the safety pin and I was relieved when he handed it over amicably. It was all rather pathetic. He was just like a small boy with a toy. I deposited the grenade in the first slit trench that I passed and, afterwards, wondered if I might not have slain a cave-dweller, as I never bothered to look.

About 4 p.m. we mustered and paraded the battalion. The camp was now a charred and smouldering ruin. Everything had gone except our weapons, ammunition and equipment. The pipes and drums; the band instruments; all our kits, everything was gone except the spirit of the regiment.

David Wilson stood next to me as the men fell in. He had lost a sword that his father and his grandfather before him had carried in the regiment. 'Well,' said David, 'I don't know, but the bloody Japs can't have any of it now and I think it's rather better that way.'

There were about fifty of all ranks on parade. We formed the men into sections, and the sections into platoons. There were some more marines to come in later on. The colonel stood in front of the remnants of the battalion and told them what they were going to do and what was expected of them. They were to stand on their positions and fight to the last man. The men had a look of grim but cheerful determination on their faces. They were going to fight; there was no doubt about that.

I thought of the immortal picture of 'The Thin Red Line', which had won my admiration since I first remembered it hanging in the nursery of my childhood; and now it hung in my own son's nursery. Here was the same battalion, the 93rd Highlanders, nearly a hundred years later. Balaclava, Singapore—Flintlocks and Feather Bonnets—Tin Hats and Tommy Guns. *Plus ça change, plus c'est la même chose.* Yes, I thought, and damn all so-called military reformers who have tried to eliminate Regimental Tradition; damn them and blast them all to hell. Let them come to Singapore and have a look at some of the units where regimental tradition didn't count; let them have a look at other regiments that had the traditions, but lacked officers, through 'milking' and battle casualties, who valued these traditions more than their own skins.

Ian Stewart remained to improvise an organisation for our administrative requirements and he ordered me to take over command of our remnants. I led the battalion through the red-hot crackling embers of the camp, out of Argyll Gate and up Holland Road, towards the line that lay a bare three miles ahead, with the whistle of shells and the crump of their explosions to speed us on our way.

David Wilson, Michael Blackwood and I marched at the head. I glanced back to watch the sections swinging forward in open file, on each side of the road. Under our battle-grimed uniforms we did at least look like soldiers. We passed some stragglers coming back from the line. One of them called out: 'Wha'-d'-yer-want to go up into that hell for;'

The Jocks looked straight to their front, marching voluntarily to attention, and never saying a word. We plugged steadily on and the crackle of musketry grew louder as we approached the line. David, Michael and I were agreeing on a joint plan of action after Singapore fell, as it was now quite obviously merely a question of time. The position we were going to occupy lay in thick jungle and it was possible that we might still be alive after the Japs had broken through. In this case, we intended to have a rendezvous, in rear of the Japs, on the Jurong River. Here we would doubtless be able to collect a *sampan* and row, by night, to the yacht club where Mike's boat, stocked with food and water, lay moored.

We were still discussing the plans when Angus Macdonald drew up alongside in a staff car.

'Haven't you heard?' he said. 'It's all been changed.' This was a frivolous *cliche* in Malaya Command.

'No, joking apart,' he added, 'General Keith Simmons has pointed out that it is absurd to send 50 odd men up to occupy a battalion sector. The Australians have reported their position as considerably better. You've to halt the battalion here and await further orders, which will come up by a liaison officer.'

We halted, cleared the road and faced outwards. This was a bit of a blow to our crusading spirit. We were keyed up for a fight and these new orders introduced a sensation of emptiness. It was an anti-climax and I suddenly felt tired.

Our new orders were to return to camp where we would be put into huts, belonging to one of the Indian battalions, that had escaped the fire. We trudged down Holland Road to the camp and, as darkness fell, the men were issued with tea and stew. As soon as accommodation was allotted they fell into the instant sleep of utter exhaustion. The brigadier had arranged for the officers to be fed in two batches at the brigade mess and I motored down in the inky blackness, with Ian, for the second sitting.

Dinner wasn't ready when we arrived, but a cold whisky and soda was going down splendidly and nobody minded the delay, except Ian who was a teetotaller. At this moment, a signaller came in, saluted and handed a message to the C. O. Ian read it with great deliberation, paused and handed it to me. The signal, which was from brigade headquarters, read: 'Comd. Argylls will report at this Headquarters immediately with two most experienced officers and N.C.O.s.' It was prefixed with a high priority.

'Oh, hell' I thought. 'Now what are they going to do with us?' I foresaw a special reconnaissance or patrol task that would necessitate another sleepless night. I really didn't feel I was physically capable of staying awake and I was ravenously hungry. Turning to Ian, I said, 'Do I come with you, or do I take over command:'

'You come with me,' said Ian. 'Now, there's no time for delay. Who is the other officer to be?'

'David,' I replied, stuffing as much cottage pie into my mouth as possible.

'I must tell you now,' said Ian, 'that this job probably takes us to Java, and will entail instructing in jungle warfare. We must have first class representatives of the regiment.'

'All right, sir. I say David. He's instructed at the O.C.T.U. and he's the only other regular, apart from Mike, who lacks David's experience.'

'Right then—you and David. Now—N.C.O.s—I think I can get P.S.M. Colvin from Sumatra. What about Nutall?'

'Nutall was wounded yesterday. I don't know how badly, but rather fancy he is not on duty. I would like to take Bing'.

We waffled on for a few minutes, and then Ian said, 'We'll go to brigade H.Q. now, and collect David and C.S.M. Bing.'

Ian went in to see the brigadier and I waited outside whilst orderlies went in search of David and the sergeant-major. Eventually Ian., the brigadier and Angus emerged.

'Well, good luck to you,' said Archie. 'You're off to Java tonight.'

We shook hands all round. Old Angus might have been seeing us off after a dinner party—the same humorous chuckle, the same quick wit and generosity. 'I give you a couple of weeks longer than us before finishing up in the cooler.'

'Goodbye—good luck—keep your wicket up!' and with these parting words, and many farewells to officers and the rank and file, we disappeared into the darkness to report at Singapore Fortress H.Q.

We sat silently in the car all feeling that, leaving the regiment like this, we were no better than rats deserting a sinking ship. Archie and Angus would look after the regiment all right. It was not intended that we should be used in the line again, so our further services with the unit would have been misplaced. All the same, the sweetness of fresh hope, which our reprieve had given to us, was embittered by the thought of those we had left behind.

At Singapore Fortress H. Q., we reported to the Operations Room. This was a bomb-proof installation, built well underground and ventilated by air-conditioning. The plant was nothing like big enough for the number of people working there, and the hot oppressive atmosphere was accentuated by the heavy vibration of the machinery.

General Keith Simmons and his staff bade us a generous farewell and we received orders to embark on board the cruiser *Durban,* which was due in any time that night. In the meantime, we went to some remote house in the town which was the headquarters of the Chinese Communists. This organisation had now been regimented into a guerrilla force under the command of a very able policeman called Dalley. The men had been armed with sawn-off shot guns and other improvised weapons and undertook the duties of fighting the Japs in the mangrove swamps on the western shores of the island. I never heard what degree of success attended their efforts, but I fear a large number were captured and summarily executed. At this house, we slept on the floor for an hour or two, in company with an odd assortment of people, and then drove to the docks.

CHAPTER 12

Out of the Darkness, Through the Fire into the Reistaffel

It must have been about 2 a.m. when *Durban* tied up and we went on board. She had been based on Singapore for quite a time and there was a very close liaison between our regiment and the ship's company. Apart from football matches and mess entertainments, the sailors sometimes came and played soldiers with us, and we took good care to see that they got their nice white suits well dirtied in jungle slime! We, on the other hand, very often attended target practice as guests of the sailors and, in consequence, were no strangers in the wardroom.

After a cup of cocoa and a sandwich I went up on deck to take a last look at Singapore. The 9.2-inch guns from Blakang Mati were firing over our heads. Away to the west there was a continuous thunder of fire from the battle front. I could vaguely discern that part of the line for which we had been destined. The moon should be just about rising, but the whole sky was blotted out by the smoke from the oil fires. The only illumination was from the countless conflagrations and the muzzle-flash of guns.

I stood silently wrapped in thought. Singapore—a shattered bastion—a burning pyre—a parody of Britain's might. Goodbye Singapore—farewell my friends. God, bless you all.

The next morning I awoke from a deep sleep, in one of the wardroom chairs, and was just contemplating a wash and a shave when the ship's alarm buzzed out *ack-ack—ack-ack—ack-ack*. The bugle sounded action stations and the ship's company moved with quick but quiet deliberation to their places of duty. Ian, David and I, together with one or two R.A.F. officers who were also passengers, were told to stay put in the wardroom.

We took up our places in easy chairs and I selected a book from the library. The first lieutenant came in and said that a Jap formation was attacking the *Empire Star*. This was one of the ships in our convoy. The *Empire Star* had brought down a couple of enemy aircraft and, in the course of the next half-hour, she suffered two or three direct hits, but was not seriously damaged.

'When the Jap aircraft start on us,' said the first lieutenant, 'you chaps want to lie down flat because this stuff,' he added tapping the side, 'doesn't keep anything out.'

We did not have to wait very long for our turn. Our port and starboard 3-inch ack-ack guns indicated when the Jap aircraft were running up to attack. *Durban's*, ack-ack armament was years out of date, and the slow dull thuds of the two 3-inch guns gave me the impression of utter impotency. The signal for adopting the horizontal position was when the ack-ack guns ceased fire, as this indicated that bomb releases would shortly take place.

I was trying to concentrate on my book, *The Riddle of the Sands*, but after about twenty-five pages I had to admit that I was not really very wrapped up in the story. The first lieutenant poked his head in from time to time and gave a running commentary on the action.

'Two more formations of nine aircraft have been spotted.'

Every time the ack-ack stopped we prostrated ourselves on the floor. The salvos of bombs were not nearly as noisy as they sounded when dropped in the open, but the feeling of claustrophobia and defencelessness made these conditions much more unpleasant than any I had previously encountered.

In the lulls, between attacks, we got up and relaxed in chairs. I failed to notice one of these and was immediately accused of 'cave-dwelling' by David.

In the next attack, there was a sickening thump which vibrated through, the whole ship and this was followed by a rattle of splinters against the ship's bottom. One direct hit and a number of near misses was the score in this assault.

Ian and I, considering discretion the better part of valour, eased under the wardroom table. I continued with *The Riddle of the Sands* and, at the end of every paragraph, checked the captain's port and starboard tactics with my oil compass.

Page 27, page 28, page 29—new chapter. The book wasn't really making any sense at all. I had to read the last two pages again—then, suddenly, there was God's own crash and a blinding flash. For a moment, I thought the wardroom had taken a direct hit and I couldn't quite understand why I was still alive. I sat up and burnt my hand on a red-hot splinter. The wardroom was still there, but the ship's side was one mass of ugly gashes and the pungent fumes of cordite permeated the whole room. We had merely taken a near miss to port. One of the R. A.F. officers had been hit in the chest by a splinter and David had taken a ricochet in the back of his head. The wall fan lay in a tangled heap on the floor, exactly where my head had been before I had moved my position. There was now quite considerable competition for a place under the table. A seaman came in and started to hammer wooden wedges into the splinter holes, to keep out the sea water.

Page 29—new chapter and more bombs. Someone called out 'Fire aft in No. 1 hatch. Send No. 3 duty party this way.' Seamen moved down the passage outside the wardroom, running out a hose. Someone called 'Gangway, please!' It was splendid to watch the quick and silent deliberation of the ship's company. There was no shouting, no wild rushing about, no blinding or swearing.

The fire was very close to the wardroom, and the prospects of being burnt alive were more than unpleasant; they were frankly frightening. If a fairy godmother had appeared and asked me whether I would take a free passage back to Singapore on a magic broomstick, I think I would have accepted the offer.

To pep up my spirits I repeated to myself the *stanzas* of Henley's *Invictus*. I had always regarded it as one of the strongest poems that has ever been written; and what colossal self-confidence.

In the fell clutch of circumstance
I have not winced nor cried aloud.
Under the bludgeonings of chance
My head is bloody, but unbow'd.

The back of David's head was bloody but mine was intact so far. If our heads were unbowed they were certainly not very far off the floor.

It matters not how strait the gate,
How charged with punishments the scroll,
I am the master of my fate:
I am the captain of my soul.

I am never able to agree with the one from last line and I found I acquired greater comfort by changing this to read:

God is the master of my fate;

I am the captain of my soul.

It would have been hot in the wardroom under normal conditions, but now, with the hatches and portholes battened down and the extra heat radiated by the fire, it was as hot as hell. I had always been a pretty useful sweater but, under the existing conditions, I was easily beating all previous records and had gone clean through every stitch of clothing. The floor was now awash with water from the fire hoses, but the fire itself was soon reported to be under control.

Bearer parties started bringing wounded men into the wardroom which was doing duty as after-sick-bay. We surfaced from under the table and assisted in making the wounded comfortable. The doctor moved about with quiet efficiency, giving a morphia injection here and dressing another man there. I was glad to have something to do but, once the wounded were settled, there was no further useful task to perform, so I moved out and took up a position in the passage, in a well-meaning attempt to get out of the way. This, however, was quite the wrong place to select as it obstructed the movement of duty parties, and I stopped an Imperial Raspberry from the first lieutenant. We had a good laugh about this afterwards as he had mistaken me for a marine.

One of the two ack-ack guns had taken a direct hit, and the crew had been killed. The other gun remained in action until the ammunition was exhausted, after which we had no defence at all.

I kept looking alternately at my book, my watch and my compass. The minutes ticked slowly past and so it went on—port—starboard—port—starboard—to the accompaniment of the whining of the stokehold fans and the periodical crash of bombs. Our course was approximately due south but we were often heading north. The revs were alternately decreased and increased and the whole ship heeled as the wheel was put over in desperate attempts to avoid the bomb patterns. How much longer had we got to stick this?

And then at about 1 p.m. it all finished. The last enemy aircraft had cleared off. The relief was intense. I found I had clenched my fists so tightly that my nails had dug into the palms of my hands. Tea was served and incidents of the action were light-heartedly narrated and discussed by the officers. I went up on deck and chatted to members of the ship's company. There was a good deal of visible damage. We had been attacked by one formation of 27 aircraft and a number of smaller formations, and the attacks had been spread out over a period of nearly five hours. We had suffered three direct hits and numbers of near misses.

Everyone was singing the praises of the captain. Apart from the skill with which he had handled his ship, his coolness and composure under enemy fire had been an inspiration to all. To have experienced an air attack at sea is an ordeal I hope not to repeat, but the conduct of these sailors in action is a privilege which I hold it an honour to have witnessed.

The next day was Friday, February 13th, and, again, at 8 a.m. the ack-ack alarm was sounded and a Jap reconnaissance machine disappeared to the north. We took up action stations and steeled ourselves for a repetition of yesterday's performance but, fortunately, nothing further happened and, by the late afternoon, we could count ourselves pretty well safe.

That evening, we berthed at Batavia and David and I were invited by the Snotties to take a noggin in the Gunroom. We had a very cheery party and you would not have thought any of these boys had been through a recent ordeal. In the middle of one of the better stories Ian poked his head in and said we were to disembark.

As we stood on the quayside Captain Cazalet came ashore unostentatiously, in the dark, to inspect some damage forward. He was spotted and someone called for three cheers. The whole ship's company crashed out in splendid unison—'Hurray!—Hurray !—Hurray!—and a Tiger-Hurray!'

There was no accommodation in Batavia and after milling around the city we finished up at the Hotel des Indes. Here we ran into a war correspondent who very kindly invited us all to dine as his guests at the Harmonic Club. The Harmonic was founded by Sir Stamford Raffles. It was an excellent club and the principal rule was that at no hour of the day or night must the bar ever close. The Dutch made all serving officers members of this club and we were most grateful for their hospitality.

That night I slept in a child's play-pen which I found in one of the passages at the Hotel des Indes. This was not really very satisfactory as the mosquitoes were plentiful and virulent and I got badly bitten. Everyone in Batavia slept inside mosquito-proof cages but the difficulty was to find a cage. The next day, who should I run into but Kenneth and Emma Selby-Walker. They invited me to share their cage provided I could produce a bed, and this I was able to do, thanks to the generosity of the American Vice-Consul's wife who lent me her husband's camp bed. Another honorary member of the Selby-Walker cage was Pug Tew who commanded *Jupiter*. Pug, being a sailor, did not bring his own bed, but we excused him this as he had just sunk a Jap submarine. We had a mutual arrangement that the first three to retire took the beds and the odd one out had to lump it. Poor Pug, I'm afraid, went down with his ship in the Battle of the Java Seas some ten days later and Kenneth made the last wireless announcement from Bandoeng before the island capitulated.

Ian now went up to Bandoeng, to report to General Wavell for instructions, and David and I were left in Batavia. 'Reistaffel' was the dish of the country. A foundation of rice is supplemented by a dozen, or so major ingredients, such as fish, meat, eggs and vegetables, and, apart from these, there are countless spices and delicacies to be added according to taste. We slogged into the 'Reistaffel' in no uncertain manner and thoroughly enjoyed the Harmonic's cuisine, after our recent surfeit of bully beef and stew.

Two days after our arrival, the fall of Singapore was announced and the Japs now started to square up for an attack on Java. It was obviously too late to start training the Dutch. Furthermore, there was no organisation for instructing and, on top of this, we had a language problem. General Wavell therefore decided we would be better employed in India where our services might well be used to assist in the Burma campaign.

We were, therefore, instructed to take ship for Ceylon and, as the message did not reach us till the ship had sailed, David, Bing and I went down to the docks the following morning and obtained a passage in a small Malayan coastal steamer which was suffering a good deal from bomb damage.

We sailed up the west coast of Sumatra and almost every evening received wireless instructions to call in at some remote bay and pick up refugees or escapees. It took ten days to reach Colombo and we were more than fortunate to escape enemy submarine or air attacks during the whole of this trip. It was as well we had overeaten in Batavia, when the going was good, for in the *Pankor* we only got one meal a day on account of a shortage in rations.

On March 2nd, we anchored in Colombo and made our way to the Galle Face Hotel. Here we met lots of Malayan evacuees and also one or two escapees, including our *padre*. The circumstances occasioned a full-blooded celebration in the form of a dinner-dance. In the middle of this party in came Pat Hayward in shorts, plimsoll

British surrender on February 15th, 1942.

shoes and a dead man's shirt, but otherwise immaculately groomed and complete with eyeglass.

That party marked the end of a broken sequence of hungry days, sleepless nights, anxious moments and the never-ending burden of responsibility which are the basic ingredients of war, and so this serves as a fitting milestone at which to end the narrative. In the concluding chapter the main causes for the fall of the fortress will be summarised.

CHAPTER 13

Reflections and Responsibilities

The fall of Singapore brought forth an outburst of indignation from the British press and public. How was it that this much-vaunted fortress had fallen so easily to the Jap aggressor?

In order of importance I would put the contributory causes in the following sequence; first and foremost, the inadequacy of our Air Force, secondly our military unpreparedness, as compared with Japanese standards, and thirdly our failure to co-ordinate all the resources of the country in the form of a united front. It is worthwhile examining these contributory causes in detail, and they appear in better perspective if the last is taken first.

Our failure to present a united front to the enemy concerns the races and communities that inhabited the peninsula and the customs and methods under which they were governed and administered. As a professional soldier, I do not consider myself qualified to deal with this subject in detail, but I will just sketch a quick impression of the country as it struck me. The main communities consisted of Europeans, Chinese, Malays and Indians. The European community was either there in an administrative capacity or else in search of wealth. The Chinese were there to exploit the country and the Indians to better their standard of living.

The Malays were an easy-going good-natured and peace-loving people, who were content to have their country run for them, provided they could continue their carefree existence. There was no common bond of love of country, or pride of race, but the whole four communities gave the impression of being loosely knit together by the ties of business interest. Money was the God. Nothing else mattered but money, and the ways in which money was acquired were, as often as not, scarcely in keeping with the accepted standards of honesty.

On top of these business communities a military force of fair size was superimposed and this military structure sat very uneasily on its foundations. There was no unity of purpose embracing the whole resources of the States and colonies and including the military forces. There was neither strength nor power, nor greatness in the Government. There was never any serious effort to prepare the country mentally or materially for totalitarian war.

These omissions had a number of consequences in the subsequent campaign. First, they permitted the Japs to carry out a series of unhampered military activities in the country before hostilities broke out. These included the work of agents on normal intelligence duties and also, I venture to say, an organisation for dumping material at selected sites for the repair of our demolitions. I can only qualify this latter assertion by quoting two incidents which are in the nature of circumstantial evidence.

First, in the withdrawal of Johore, a lorry, blinding down the road, detonated an important bridge at Seremban which left 12th Brigade on the wrong side. In the matter of a few hours the Sappers had mended the bridge with material collected on the spot. Secondly, on the Temerloh raid I heard railway engines working on the track between Taiping and Kuala Kangsar. The rolling stock must have all come from Thailand and, in view of the fact that we had blown all the bridges between Jitra and Kuala Kangsar, including two major demolitions over the Krian and Muda Rivers, I fail to see how the Japs could have reopened the line in this short space of time, unless the material was already dumped.

The second consequence of our civil omissions was the failure of our denial and destruction plans. This enabled the Japs to exploit local resources in the shape of coastal and native craft, vehicles, cycles, food, petrol and oil and other valuable military stores. In this respect the services, and more particularly the R.A.F., must accept their full share of blame. The main point about destruction and denial that struck me, was the lack of co-operation between the civil administration and the services. A further regrettable failure in co-operation concerns the policy of the Local Volunteer Forces. I think it is no exaggeration to say that, on their existing organisation, they were totally unfit for war, yet all the material existed for the formation of a first-class Corps of Guides which would have been an invaluable component to our regular forces.

The last and most important consequence of our civil omissions was the breakdown of labour in the face of the enemy's fire. This had far-reaching effects, even to the fighting in the forward areas.

I make no claim that the foregoing paragraphs give anything approaching a comprehensive commentary on what might be termed the people's front, but I think that the application of our democratic colonial policy was bound to result in our failure to produce a united effort in time of war and that this state was aggravated by an absence of high-grade men in our Malayan Colonial Service. All the same, these were merely contributory causes to our defeat and the main reasons were military ones.

For a fuller and better appreciation of the people's front, I would recommend Ian Morrison's *Malayan Postscript,* which I had the good fortune to re-adjust before submitting this book for publication. *Malayan Postscript* struck me as being a remarkably fair and balanced commentary and read in conjunction with this account, I think the two books give a moderately comprehensive background to all aspects of the campaign.

Turning now to the purely military factors, we have already seen that the policy of the defence scheme was to hold Malaya by means of the R.A.F. and that once we lost air superiority Singapore was doomed. The fact remains that the Japs dominated the air from the very first day of the war and our failure to provide sufficient aircraft and crews to meet the actual Jap scale of attack was, to my mind, the direct cause of our defeat.

This failure may be accounted for in one of three ways. First, the aircraft may not have been available without denuding either Great Britain or the Middle East of their minimum requirements; and Whitehall may have appreciated that it was better to lose Singapore than Alexandria or London. However, in this case, it may fairly be asked why did we decide to hold Malaya with the R.A.F. ? I think the answer to this one is that Singapore could only be held, against a land-based attack, by keeping the Japs outside the radius of Fighter support, which virtually dictated the forward policy of fighting on the frontiers. A forward policy would necessitate either a lot more aeroplanes or a lot more troops and the former were no doubt easier to find than the latter.

I think a second possible reason why sufficient aircraft were not available was that the producers had not turned out the numbers for which they had contracted.

A third solution may have been due to over confidence in the A.B.C.D. asset-freezing front and in the belief that the Japs had been forced into such a state of national bankruptcy that they would only resort to arms as a last act of national *hart kari*. We must have seen Japan as a second rate power, encircled by an iron chain of united nations, in which there was no weak link otherwise the spirit of easy optimism that prevailed is unaccountable. There is no doubt that easy optimism did exist, and if anyone should doubt this contention they have only to read the official proclamation that was issued to the troops and the civilians on the day that hostilities broke out, and compare it with what Mr. Churchill had to say when France capitulated.

Anyhow, as the course of the subsequent campaign proved, the Japs had calculated every factor in the Pacific defensive layout and they took to arms under conditions when they had every reason to be confident of initial success and exploitation. I think it was unfortunate that the people of Malaya and the British public were given to understand that Singapore was impregnable.

In summary, therefore, the defeat of the R.A.F. was either due to shortage of aircraft, from productive or strategic reasons, or else because our intelligence was at fault and we imagined that we had sufficient aircraft for the task, and, as a result of these deficiencies in men and material, I venture to say that seldom have our troops been called upon to fight under more unfavourable conditions than those that we came up against in. Malaya. On the other hand, however, there is no doubt that, had our fighting services been better trained and prepared, we could have put up a far better show than we did. Singapore would still have fallen in the end but there is no reason why it should not have gone down in history as a glorious page in the records of our army.

As far as military unpreparedness is concerned, I shall confine my observations to the army, but these remarks all apply in lesser or greater degree to the R.A.F. In the first place, it must be appreciated that we had to contend with a number of unfavourable conditions. Troops had to be kept deployed in their battle areas, and it was not easy to concentrate formations at will for collective training. Practice ammunition was not available and the climatic conditions were lowering. The majority of troops lived in semi-deployment, under the rubber trees, so that the camps would not afford vulnerable bombing targets, and the dark, rank, sultry oppressive atmosphere must be experienced to be believed. It just drained all vitality and effectively eliminated those qualities of mental and physical alertness which are a *sine qua non* of every fighting soldier.

Had the danger of bombing the semi-deployment camps been accepted, and had these camps been built on airy hillsides, I think the general morale and health would have been three times better. In our military training we had been taught to assess the morale to the physical as three is to one, but when it came to the practical application of our knowledge we reversed the formula.

Under these conditions, it is not surprising that the very clever subversive propaganda, which the Japs sowed amongst our Indian troops, should take root. Apart from Indian troops, though, all units were at some time or another, or to a greater or lesser extent, found lacking in morale and this I attribute to the democratic principles on which the youth of our Empire have been educated. It is not enough to teach a man to think for himself, because, to quote Rudyard Kipling, *'unfortunately to attain this virtue, he has to pass through the phase of thinking of himself, and that is misdirected genius'*. In our post-war educational policy and in our projected youth movements I hope that we will bear this lesson in mind.

Troops with a purely democratic education are at a great disadvantage when the odds are against them and, unless they have had the privilege of being trained in a strictly disciplined regiment, the chances are that they will not stand firm. We are a democratic nation, but how many of us realise that we owe our existence to the security afforded us by the disciplined units of the fighting services, and in a disciplined unit democracy has no part. The lesson of all this seems to be moderation in all things and a time and place for everything; including democracy.

So much for our morale unpreparedness. On the material side the paramount factor was our failure to produce jungle trained troops. The reinforcements that went up to fight did so in green ignorance and it is small wonder that they were unable to give a better account of themselves. Our Commands and Staffs worked hard enough, but the point is that their work was almost entirely misdirected, and this I attribute to our whole pre-war system which was academic as opposed to practical, and the reason it was academic was because the British taxpayer would not produce the necessary monetary votes to make it anything else.

Every soldier is familiar with the Duke of Wellington's *dictum* that there are no bad men, but only bad officers. I have often wondered why the Duke, being a statesman, did not go a step further and add that there are no bad officers, only bad politicians. The renaissance in our army which started, curiously enough, with Mr. Churchill's advent to power, and which was eagerly awaited for so long by the majority of our regular officers would seem to establish this theory, and, if further proof is required, an examination of national military records in current history gives further strength to the argument.

The fact remains that in the Malayan campaign we were outclassed by an Asiatic nation of an inferior intellectual standard, in military preparedness, in manoeuvre and in actual fighting. The Japanese troops were first class and their major tactics were brilliant. Not only were they well trained, but, as a result of practical study, they had originated tactics specifically suited for jungle fighting. They showed themselves to be no mere imitators. From top to bottom they were intensely practical, and this included not only the tactical conceptions of their Commands and Staffs, but also their application of fire, their engineering and field works and their exploitation of local resources.

They turned to full account their ability to live hard and to live on the country. They marched through jungle and mangrove like wild beasts. They sat motionless for hours in trees or in flooded *padi* fields. They accepted casualties, they fought fast, they fought dangerously. Generally speaking, they fought cleanly. Our hospitals were not bombed, and the weight of their air attacks were confined, almost entirely, to military objectives. Credit must be given where credit is due, and we must admit that our military forces were thrashed by the Japs in every respect. That does not mean to say that the Jap soldier is invincible. He has his weaknesses as well as his assets, and we can and shall beat him man for man in the field, and brain for brain in organisation and training.

These I think were the contributory causes that brought about the most ignominious defeat that Britain has suffered since the loss of the American Colonies, and may it be seen that a share in the responsibility for this defeat must be borne by almost every section of the public. The object of recriminations is to prevent repetitions, so let each one draw his own particular lesson so far as his own duties or his responsibilities as a member of the electorate are concerned. Above all let the cautious and conventional time-servers, who have not the interest of the country at heart, be cast out.

God Save The King.

LEONAUR

ALSO FROM LEONAUR
AVAILABLE IN SOFTCOVER OR HARDCOVER WITH DUST JACKET

THE 9TH—THE KING'S (LIVERPOOL REGIMENT) IN THE GREAT WAR 1914 - 1918 *by Enos H. G. Roberts*—Mersey to mud—war and Liverpool men.

THE GAMBARDIER *by Mark Severn*—The experiences of a battery of Heavy artillery on the Western Front during the First World War.

FROM MESSINES TO THIRD YPRES *by Thomas Floyd*—A personal account of the First World War on the Western front by a 2/5th Lancashire Fusilier.

THE IRISH GUARDS IN THE GREAT WAR - VOLUME 1 *by Rudyard Kipling*—Edited and Compiled from Their Diaries and Papers—The First Battalion.

THE IRISH GUARDS IN THE GREAT WAR - VOLUME 1 *by Rudyard Kipling*—Edited and Compiled from Their Diaries and Papers—The Second Battalion.

ARMOURED CARS IN EDEN *by K. Roosevelt*—An American President's son serving in Rolls Royce armoured cars with the British in Mesopatamia & with the American Artillery in France during the First World War.

CHASSEUR OF 1914 *by Marcel Dupont*—Experiences of the twilight of the French Light Cavalry by a young officer during the early battles of the great war in Europe.

TROOP HORSE & TRENCH *by R.A. Lloyd*—The experiences of a British Lifeguardsman of the household cavalry fighting on the western front during the First World War 1914-18.

THE EAST AFRICAN MOUNTED RIFLES *by C.J. Wilson*—Experiences of the campaign in the East African bush during the First World War.

THE LONG PATROL *by George Berrie*—A Novel of Light Horsemen from Gallipoli to the Palestine campaign of the First World War.

THE FIGHTING CAMELIERS *by Frank Reid*—The exploits of the Imperial Camel Corps in the desert and Palestine campaigns of the First World War.

STEEL CHARIOTS IN THE DESERT *by S. C. Rolls*—The first world war experiences of a Rolls Royce armoured car driver with the Duke of Westminster in Libya and in Arabia with T.E. Lawrence.

WITH THE IMPERIAL CAMEL CORPS IN THE GREAT WAR *by Geoffrey Inchbald*—The story of a serving officer with the British 2nd battalion against the Senussi and during the Palestine campaign.

LEONAUR

ALSO FROM LEONAUR
AVAILABLE IN SOFTCOVER OR HARDCOVER WITH DUST JACKET

THE FALL OF THE MOGHUL EMPIRE OF HINDUSTAN *by H. G. Keene*—By the beginning of the nineteenth century, as British and Indian armies under Lake and Wellesley dominated the scene, a little over half a century of conflict brought the Moghul Empire to its knees.

LADY SALE'S AFGHANISTAN *by Florentia Sale*—An Indomitable Victorian Lady's Account of the Retreat from Kabul During the First Afghan War.

THE CAMPAIGN OF MAGENTA AND SOLFERINO 1859 *by Harold Carmichael Wylly*—The Decisive Conflict for the Unification of Italy.

FRENCH'S CAVALRY CAMPAIGN *by J. G. Maydon*—A Special Correspondent's View of British Army Mounted Troops During the Boer War.

CAVALRY AT WATERLOO *by Sir Evelyn Wood*—British Mounted Troops During the Campaign of 1815.

THE SUBALTERN *by George Robert Gleig*—The Experiences of an Officer of the 85th Light Infantry During the Peninsular War.

NAPOLEON AT BAY, 1814 *by F. Loraine Petre*—The Campaigns to the Fall of the First Empire.

NAPOLEON AND THE CAMPAIGN OF 1806 *by Colonel Vachée*—The Napoleonic Method of Organisation and Command to the Battles of Jena & Auerstädt.

THE COMPLETE ADVENTURES IN THE CONNAUGHT RANGERS *by William Grattan*—The 88th Regiment during the Napoleonic Wars by a Serving Officer.

BUGLER AND OFFICER OF THE RIFLES *by William Green & Harry Smith*—With the 95th (Rifles) during the Peninsular & Waterloo Campaigns of the Napoleonic Wars.

NAPOLEONIC WAR STORIES *by Sir Arthur Quiller-Couch*—Tales of soldiers, spies, battles & sieges from the Peninsular & Waterloo campaigns.

CAPTAIN OF THE 95TH (RIFLES) *by Jonathan Leach*—An officer of Wellington's sharpshooters during the Peninsular, South of France and Waterloo campaigns of the Napoleonic wars.

RIFLEMAN COSTELLO *by Edward Costello*—The adventures of a soldier of the 95th (Rifles) in the Peninsular & Waterloo Campaigns of the Napoleonic wars.

9 781782 826439